Publications of the
Association of Ancient Historians

The purpose of the monograph series is to survey the state of the current scholarship in various areas of ancient history.

Other publications by the Association

The Coming of the Greeks

James T. Hooker

University College, London

Published for the
Association of Ancient Historians

Regina Books
Claremont, California

© 1999 by Association of Ancient Historians

Library of Congress Cataloging-in-Publication Data

Hooker, J. T.
    The coming of the Greeks / James T. Hooker.
        p.   cm.
    "Published for the Association of Ancient Historians"
    Includes bibliographical references.
    ISBN 0-941690-88-1 (cloth). – ISBN 0-941690-89-x (pbk.)
    1. Greeks—Origin. 2. Greece—History—To 146 B.C. 3.Archaeology
    and history—Greece. 4. Greek language. I. Title.
DF220.H64 1999
938'.01—dc21   98-47936
                                     CIP

Co-published by arrangement with the
Association of Ancient Historians

Regina Books

Post Office Box 280
Claremont, California 91711
Tel: (909) 624-8466 / Fax (909) 626-1345

Manufactured in the United States of America.

CONTENTS

INTRODUCTION

Neither the subject nor author of this volume requires lengthy introduction. Even Greeks of the Classical Age worried about "the coming of the Greeks" and, to the present day, an explanation satisfactory to all remains elusive. James Hooker tackled the major issues associated with the question in these three essays: the first was published in *Historia* (1976), the third in *Minos* (1989) and the second presented at a conference but not published. His analysis of these issues is so sensible and cogent that gathering the three discussions in a single volume will benefit many students of history, classics, historical linguistics, and archaeology.

The insight stems from James' breadth of interest: a member of the Department of Greek at University College, London for much of his professional career, his work ranged from Linear B to Classical Greek and included matters archaeological and historical as well as philological. By way of example, his *Scripta Minora*, collected and edited by his wife Sheila Hooker and his friend and colleague Patrick Considine (A.M. Hakkert, Amsterdam, 1996), contains 721 pages of essays on Minoan, Mycenaean, Homeric, and Classical Greek subjects. As the volume grew larger and larger, the articles on the coming of the Greeks were not included, in part because all had not been published.

His firm grasp of language and archaeology suited James Hooker to deal with the problems surrounding the arrival of Greek speakers in Greece inasmuch as the evidence of both physical remains and linguistic development form the core of the subject.

The significance of language relationships was proposed in the late eighteenth century by Sir William Jones, an orientalist as well as an English judge serving in India. Knowing Sanskrit in addition to Latin and Greek, he observed that the structure of all three was so similar that they must have sprung from a common source, now lost. Following his lead, other students of language added more languages to the list of related tongues. (The list includes Italic, Germanic, Balto-Slavic, Greek, Celtic, Armenian, Albanian, Indo-Iranian—all currently spoken—and Anatolian and Tocarian, now extinct). Their distribution suggested a collective name, given by Thomas Young in 1813: Indo-European. Study of the historical development of these languages and reconstruction of the original Indo-European language (known as Proto-Indo-European or PIE) became the field of historical linguistics. Study of how languages change and the relationships that exist between cognate languages provides no necessary link between language groups and particular cultures in certain regions at specific times.

That issue stems from two additional questions: where was the Proto-Indo-European homeland and how did the Indo-European languages come to exist in an area stretching from India to western Europe? Since the dispersal occurred in prehistoric times, no documentary evidence exists to provide answers. Hence, those seeking solutions must turn to the evidence of prehistory offered by archaeology. The artifacts of a group of people may yield information about movement of that group as well as define certain of its cultural characteristics. In fact, language itself may support archaeology in that names of places and objects known in earlier times and other locations can be "fossilized" in a language or in a place, to be preserved long after its speakers have moved to new regions and are using new objects. A variety of tree, a certain animal, a kind of pot can help to identify the place of origin and the final abode of those who originally knew or invented it.

As scholars we would like to know when a group of people speaking one of the early Indo-European languages moved to another area. It is not easy to satisfy this curiosity. Physical objects can be dated but only approximately. The rate of linguistic change is not constant. Only the brave will tackle challenges of pots "walking" across vast distances, "speaking" a language that is changing at an unknown rate from the reconstructed language of their postulated homeland.

James Hooker was brave in confronting all the issues. Each essay explores an important argument proposed by a specific scholar or scholars. The first examines the conclusion of Ernst Grumach that the Greeks entered the Aegean in a single movement at a late date, moving from the Danube basin. Essay two scrutinizes hypotheses of Marija Gimbutas and Colin Renfew that seek to explain both the cause of dispersal and its source. In the final article, he confronts the argument of Robert Drews that traces the use of horse-drawn chariots in the ancient Near East and eastern Mediterranean as an indicator of the coming of the Greeks.

In every case, Hooker points to strengths as well as weaknesses, offers copious references, and scrutinizes without malice. A sign of the nature of his discussions is that the authors whose hypotheses he examined who are still living have persisted in their efforts, adding to and refining their positions.[1]

To scholars as brave and able as the subjects of James Hooker's scrutiny, these introductory words are unnecessary and simplistic. However, in the hope that this volume will be valuable to readers whose interests

---

[1] Robert Drews, "PIE Speakers and PA Speakers", *The Journal of Indo-European Studies* 25 (1997) 153-177; Colin Renfrew, "World linguistic diversity and farming dispersals," in R. Blench and M. Spriggs edd., *Archaeology and Language I: theoretical and methodological orientations* (Routledge: London and New York, 1997) 82-90.

are in different areas, the context may be of some assistance.

Many people have assisted this collection. A list begins with Sheila Hooker whose enthusiasm when we walked the moors near her Cornish home propelled it from idea to activity. Next in line is Patrick Considine who encouraged and offered assistance. The Seventh Aegean Prehistory Conference in Liège in April 1998 was an ideal occasion to learn whether the plan would be welcomed by others whose work is closely allied to this issue: not a person at the meeting reacted negatively. In fact, support resulted in a subvention for publication from the Institute for Aegean Prehistory, thanks especially to the efficient shepherding of Philip Betancourt. The volume's "logo" came from the same meeting: the drawing of the cylinder from Kazarma (CMS V 585) done by Paul Rehak was offered by John Younger and Paul Rehak in the aftermath of conference.

Gaining permission to reprint was the next step. Sheila Hooker gave her permission to publish the third essay. Replies came immediately from Alexander F. Wensler on behalf of *Historia* granting permission to reprint and from José Melena on behalf of *Minos* with formal permission to reprint. Dr. Melena wrote "it would be very useful to have the three issues under the same cover and…this is a way to pay honor to the late James."

The conversion of the original text to an electronic version began with scanning undertaken by Shawn

Ross. It required multiple readings to correct errors created in the process of conversion and the careful eye of Suzanne Martin caught the final problems before text was returned to printed form by Mark Dodge of Regina Books under the direction of Richard D. Burns, president and publisher of Regina. Susanne Young's command of historical linguistics caught, and corrected, many flaws in the original words of this short introduction.

I extend thanks to all who have assisted so readily and with such enthusiasm. That response speaks to the qualities of the author of the essays. James Hooker was indeed a brilliant scholar. He was also as thoughtful toward other people as he was in his scholarship, a person you would plan a detour in order to visit (as John Younger often did en route from the United States to Greece). I count it a blessing to have known James Hooker as friend as well as model of scholarly endeavor.

Carol G. Thomas

I

THE COMING OF THE GREEKS—I

INTRODUCTION

Towards the end of his life, the late Ernst Grumach brought the formidable powers of his mind to bear on a long-standing problem, the nature and date of the 'coming of the Greeks', which is the title of two papers published post-humously in the *Bulletin of the John Rylands Library* in 1968 and 1969. I shall refer here to the continuous pagination of the reprint dated 1969. In his preface to the reprint, M.S.F. Hood emphasizes that it should be considered as a document of work in progress and in no sense the final, definitive utterance of a great scholar on an important matter. My respect for Grumach, and my indebtedness to him, are very great; and it is certainly in no carping spirit that I make the following, admittedly rather negative, remarks on his methods and conclusions. It seems a better compliment to his memory to use his argument as the starting-point of a fertile debate than to accept his opinion slavishly and uncritically.

As we should expect, Grumach discusses with clarity and succinctness the rival theories about the coming of the Greeks. The most venerable of these, and still to-day the most widely held, identifies the first Greeks as the destroyers of the native culture of the Greek mainland at the end of the Early Helladic III period or, if Caskey's revised dating is accepted, at the end of Early Helladic II. Palmer and Heubeck, for their part, take a different view and believe that an Anatolian language, not Greek, was brought to the mainland c. 1900 B.C. and that the speakers of the Greek language did not arrive until the Mycenaean period. All these theories, as Grumach shows, are open to very serious objections; and he accordingly devotes the greater part of his paper to arguments in favour of what seems to him the only possible date left for the immigration of the Greeks, namely Late Helladic IIIc, after the destruction of the major Mycenaean settlements.

It seems right, before criticizing Grumach's own position, to mention some respects in which his argumentation seems soundly based. It is, in the first place, wholly admirable that he makes use of three kinds of relevant evidence—linguistic, archaeological, and mythological—which he tries to inter-relate. That, certainly, is the only means by which final answers to these problems, if indeed they are ever arrived at, will be attained. Again, he is quite justified in pointing out how inconclusive and ambiguous is the witness of the Linear B tablets. Grumach, unlike myself, does not accept the validity of Ventris' decipherment of the Linear B script; but I agree with him that the dialectal affinities of Mycenaean Greek, as recorded in Linear B documents, are much too obscure to be used as clear evidence for the migration of this or that 'wave' of Greek-speakers. Those who believe that Ventris achieved a convincing decipherment of Linear B naturally believe also, without further argument, that Greek-speakers were already present in Greece, in greater or smaller numbers, by the time that the earliest surviving Linear B texts were written, c. 1375 B.C. (I find incredible the notion of Hampl, to which Grumach devotes some attention, that a belief in the correctness of Ventris' decipherment can be reconciled with a belief in the arrival of the Greeks after the end of the Mycenaean epoch.) However, I have decided not to regard this question as prejudged but to meet Grumach on his own ground and to consider his argument for a late arrival of the Greeks without taking Ventris' decipherment into account. I shall therefore assume, for the time being, that there is no direct evidence for the Greek language until historical times.

I begin with a matter of methodology and pose the question (which I am afraid Grumach never considers) whether it is legitimate to think in terms of the 'coming of the Greeks' as a single movement which can be marked off temporally and spatially from other migrations. Of course, Grumach is only one of many scholars who thought in such terms; and few, if any, of them have ever found it necessary to say what reasons have impelled them to regard the first arrival of the Greeks as an invasion rather than as, what is just as

likely in theory, a process of diffusion. It is worth
bearing in mind that in his first major contribution to
the subject Kretschmer reckoned with a long period,
perhaps extending over several centuries, between the
'pre-Greek' and 'Greek' areas and thought in terms not
of migration but of a gradual expansion southwards
into the Balkan peninsula.[1] Speaking from the
archaeological point of view, Schachermeyr has
reminded us that one population may be infiltrated by
another without leaving traces in the material record.[2]
The assumption of a single arrival of Greeks involves a
further assumption (not by any means so self-evident
that its probability should not be established by
argument) that 'Greeks' already existed as a separate
people on their arrival in Europe, bearing presumably
all the necessary marks of 'Greekness' which would
enable them to be recognized as such. This, I take it, is
the assumption underlying such words of Grumach as
these (p. 11): "it has long been recognized that certain
areas of meaning are particularly affected by pre-
Greek loan-words; and this permits us to make certain
deductions about the cultural level of the Greeks on
their arrival in Greece and about their cultural
dependence upon the pre-Greek population." Yet, as is
well known, Myres once devoted a fascinating book to

---

[1] *Einleitung in die Geschichte der griechischen Sprache*
(Göttingen 1896) 407.

[2] *Atti e memorie del I° Congresso Internazionale di Micenologia* I
(Rome 1968) 297-298.

the question *Who Were the Greeks?*—a question he could not answer satisfactorily in several hundred pages; but the very size of his book should serve as a warning not to argue about such matters as the time of the Greeks' arrival or what skills they did or did not possess, when we are as far as ever from discovering who the 'Greeks' were. I notice that the same point is made by R. A. McNeal in an article which accurately charts the many wrong turnings which have been taken but is not so helpful as to indicate the right road.[3]

I shall now critically examine, in order, the arguments adduced by Grumach in support of his contention (linguistic evidence for Greek intrusion into the Aegean at a late date; the history of the Greek dialects; the domicile of the Greeks before they entered the Aegean area) and then, in conclusion, scrutinize a body of evidence to which Grumach pays little attention but which seems to me important and which, on the whole, tells against him.

LINGUISTIC EVIDENCE

Grumach begins by discussing the nature of loan-words in the Greek language. "Pre-Greek loan-words are found above all in the spheres of house-building (particularly where stone-masonry is involved) and household utensils, trade and commerce, war, hunting and fishing, physical culture and luxury, food and

---

[3] *Antiquity* 46 (1972) 19-28.

cooking, religion and ceremony, music, dancing and games" (p. 11). And again: "the majority of these words obviously belong to the same substratum layer as the place-names I have mentioned—that is to say, to the layer which the Greeks suppressed at the time of their arrival in Greece. This proves that the Greeks migrated against the trend of civilization" (p. 12).

Several arguments can be urged against this view.

Despite his own *caveat* at p. 12 ("we cannot know whether *all* these loan-words came from one and the same language"), Grumach in practice regards the whole class of 'architectural' words (βλῆτρον, γεῖσον, γέφυρα, θριγκός, καμάρα, μέγαρον, πλίνθος, πύργος) and also the whole class of 'ceramic' words (ἄμβιξ, ἀρύβαλλος, βῖκος, δέπας, κάμινος, κάνθαρος, κελέβη, κέραμος, κισσύβιον, κώθων, λήκυθος, φιάλη) as elements taken over, as they stood, by a lower civilization from a higher.

There is, however, no reason to believe that all these words were taken over at one and the same time, from one and the same substrate language. Such a belief, which is quite pervasive in the hand-books, (whether in implicit or explicit form), involves us in a serious error: an error it is necessary to correct at the very outset of the inquiry. The fact that 'architectural' and 'ceramic' words respectively relate to a particular sphere of activity does not speak in favour of their *linguistic* homogeneity—unless, indeed, one reckons with the existence of a separate, identifiable 'Pelasgian' language with phonetic laws of its own; and of this (I am happy to say) there is no inkling in Grumach's work. If the 'architectural' and the 'ceramic' words cited later by Grumach, are put into a list (see Appendix), their sheer promiscuity at once becomes evident. They comprise a rag-bag of words with totally disparate origins. Even if any respectable reason had been adduced for putting on all fours words which date from the *Iliad* and words attested first in the Hellenistic or even the Roman period, a superficial examination of the list itself dispels any illusion that its components all belong to the same linguistic stratum. There are, it is true, a large number of words for which no convincing etymology has been suggested in Greek or Indo-European terms. I do not myself believe that, for this reason alone, all such words can be assigned to one 'Mediterranean substrate'; but it is quite possible that some of them should be assigned. But in the minority, there appear words which are susceptible of explanation within the boundaries of Greek (ἀρύβαλλος, βλῆτρον), or at least of Indo-European. It is possible that some even of the words which are difficult of explanation in Greek or Indo-European terms derive not from a Mediterranean substrate (which is a purely hypothetical construction and which perhaps never existed as a linguistic entity), but from a Semitic language, e.g. βῖκος, κάνθαρος, πλίνθος. It would be arbitrary to rule out the possibility of a Semitic origin for other words as well.[4]

It is hard to agree with Grumach that the linguistic and the archaeological evidence converges, in respect either of architecture or of pottery. Grumach quotes Desborough's words as if they supported his case: "following on the densely-populated Mycenaean Greece, and its splendid architectural achievements, one must accept not only a serious drop in population at this time, but also an almost complete loss of the ability to build in stone" (p. 13). Since it is agreed that after the destruction of the Mycenaean citadels the inhabitants of the Greek mainland displayed little or no interest for several generations in the craft of building in stone, this chronological gap has serious implications for Grumach's argument, for it means that the 'first Greeks' who (according to him) superseded the Mycenaeans had no reason at all to master the vocabulary of architectural terms. If they did not learn, or at least did not practise, the art of stone-masonry until much later, why should they have taken over, on their first arrival, terms relating to building in stone?[5]

The position with regard to ceramic terminology is different. "This too," says Grumach, "is an important body of evidence, since it shows that the Greeks at the time of their arrival took over to a very considerable extent the pottery of the land they occupied" (p. 13).

---

[4] O. Szemerényi, *JHS* 94 (1974) 144-157.

[5] Cf. F.J. Tritsch, *Atti* (n. 2) 315.

He takes account of the absence of any appreciable break in the development of mainland pottery during Late Helladic IIIc and sub-Mycenaean; and he rightly observes that this circumstance in itself does not exclude the possibility that a new people invaded Greece, began by using the native pottery, and eventually manufactured it themselves. But later in the same paragraph this possibility has become a certainty: "here we see that another of the migrating tribes of this period actually took over the Mycenaean pottery in their new home, exactly as must have happened in the case of the Greeks" (p. 14). Throughout this part of his paper, Grumach is concerned to show a people of low cultural attainments suddenly faced with the vocabulary of a much higher civilization and absorbing its technical terms into their own language. Although that explanation is, in theory, plausible in the field of stone-masonry (where, however, as we saw, other considerations told heavily against Grumach's hypothesis), it is incredible in respect of pottery. How is it possible to believe in a body of migrants at the end of the Bronze Age who were completely unacquainted with the art of making pottery: migrants, in other words, who had no words of their own for 'potter', 'potter's earth', 'kiln', and the like? If such a degree of ignorance is unbelievable, it follows that, if the Greeks really arrived for the first time at the end of the Bronze Age, they would have had no need of some at least of the terms which Grumach alleges they took over from the native population.

Further words are adduced as pre-Greek relics at p. 14. These are terms relating to political and social organization such as ἄναξ, βασιλεύς, δοῦλος, εἰρήνη, ἑρμηνεύς, λαός, πρεσβευτής, πρύτανις, τύραννος. Grumach believes that this terminology belongs to the Mycenaean world, upon which the Greeks imposed their own system of clan-groups or φρατρίαι. Although the concept of the φρατρία does seem to belong to a later epoch than, say, the ἄναξ or the βασιλεύς, and although the word has transparent Indo-European cognates in *fräter, bhrätar-* etc., we recall on what a dubious assumption Grumach's argument rests. It is not enough to oppose a word of undoubted Indo-European origin (φρατρία) with words (ἄναξ, βασιλεύς, etc.) which cannot be shown positively to be Indo-European. It is true, as Andrewes has shown, that when the institution of the φρατρία is mentioned by Homer (B 362-363) it is relevant to that passage only; it is not referred to again, and it has all the appearance of an isolated term which is inconsistent with its surroundings.[6] But, even if we can easily admit that φρατρία has been adopted into Greek more recently than ἄναξ or βασιλεύς, and that it does refer to a more complex social system than the one usually assumed by Homer, we are still very far from having shown that is a Greek innovation while ἄναξ and so forth are pre-Greek terms. When Grumach says that "this line of inquiry, therefore, also

---

[6] *Hermes* 89 (1961) 129-140.

serves to confirm that the Greeks entered upon the inheritance of the Mycenaean world and took over forms of political and social organization from the Mycenaeans" (p. 15), he takes for granted the very fact which is at issue, namely that ἄναξ etc. belong to a pre-Greek stratum. It is true that the Greek language presents a remarkable lacuna at the point where we might expect to find a word for 'king' cognate with Latin *rēx*, Irish *rí*, and Sanskrit *rāj-*. Given this fact in isolation, we could suggest (but then only as one, not the only, possibility) that, unlike the lndo-European-speakers to the east and the west, the Greeks had found pre-Greek terms for kingship and other institutions so well established in the areas to which they had migrated that they forthwith used these terms to the exclusion of the words they had inherited from Indo-European. The difficulty with such an explanation is that it has to be invented to account for the situation in Greece alone; whereas, as is well known, it is *only* in India and the Italo-Celtic area that the *reg-* stem is used for 'king'. This state of affairs is explained quite satisfactorily by Vendryes, who supposes that it was only at the western and eastern extremities of the Indo-European world that the most archaic institution of Indo-European kingship survived and, with it, the Indo-European word for 'king'; elsewhere, the different Indo-European language-groups used new words for the institution, presumably because the institution itself was different in character.[7]

Grumach devotes a paragraph to a very puzzling item of the Homeric vocabulary: the verb ὀπυίω. It is impossible to see in Homer's ὀπυίω a meaning other than that of γαμέω, a word which he also uses. (There is no trace in Homer of the purely sexual meaning of the word, which occurs sometimes in later Greek: in fact, at Z 268 and Π 178 it refers specifically to formal marriage). Grumach accepts the usual connection of ὀπυίω with Etruscan *puia*, 'woman' or 'wife,'. He suggests that the word was taken from Lemnos to Italy at the time of the Sea Peoples' movements: movements in which, according in Grumach, the Greeks also were involved. ὀπυίω would then have had its origin in marriages between Greek men and non-Greek women, such as are attested in the legendary union of Argonauts with Lemnian women (Pindar *Pyth.* 4. 251 f.; Ap. Rhod. 1. 853 f.). Grumach's further conclusion is that this foreign word was taken into Greek "through the language of the mothers, who bought up the next generation," while the Indo-European synonym was retained by the fathers (p. 17). In constructing his argument in this fashion, Grumach has again pondered one, but only one, possibility. There were undoubtedly movements of population on a large scale at and after the end of the thirteenth century B.C.; but whether these

---

[7] *MSL* 20 (1918) 269.

movements involved a migration from the east into
Greece is precisely what Grumach is trying to
establish. On the other hand, everybody agrees that
there were migrations in the opposite direction, from
the Greek mainland across the Aegean to Asia Minor.
Since the word appears first to our knowledge in a
poem composed in Ionia, is not the most likely
hypothesis that (if it was picked up in Lemnos at all) it
was taken not westward directly to Greece but
eastward to the Greek settlements in Anatolia, where
eventually it formed one of the large number of
metrical variants so useful to the Homeric bard?
ὀπυίω, like the other items of vocabulary mentioned
by Grumach under this heading, offers no certain or
unambiguous support for his proposition that the
Greek language was not introduced into Europe before
the Late Helladic IIIc period.

The observation that the immigrant Greeks
preserved to a considerable extent the vocabulary and
structure of their old language "can only be explained
on the assumption that the Greeks came into contact
with the earlier population of the Aegean area at a late
date" (p. 19). In Grumach's opinion, this conclusion is
confirmed by a comparison of the situation in Greece
with that in Anatolia. The grammatical structure of
Hittite and its related languages is impoverished by
contact with Homeric Greek. Grumach explains this
difference by supposing that, after their incursion into
Anatolia (c.2000 B.C.?), the Hittites had lost many
Indo-European features from their language (for

example distinction between masculine and feminine, the aorist system, and the optative) under the powerful influence of the native substrate language. The fact that Greek suffered no such impoverishment suggests to Grumach that the Greeks could not have been in contact with the Aegean substrate for nearly as long as the Hittites were in contact with the Anatolian substrate and that, in consequence, we have here a further argument in favor of a late date for the intrusion of the Greeks.

The following comments may be made on this argument. If Grumach is right, and the Greeks did not arrive in Europe until about 1200 B.C., the chronological gap between that event and the probable date of the Homeric poems (about 500 years) is much the same as that between the arrival of the Hittites in Anatolia and the first Hittite documents we possess. How is it, then, that the respective languages are so different from each other? It cannot be, as Grumach seems to imply, because Hittite had been under the influence of a substrate for much longer than Greek. We would have to suggest, rather, that the substrate in Anatolia was very different in character from the Aegean substrate; but at this point we are in danger of losing touch with reality, since the structure of the Anatolian substrate is very obscure, and that of the Aegean completely unknown. It is clear that altogether too much has been made of the influence which various substrate languages exercised upon the Indo-European dialects. That they may have had some influence cannot be denied, but they should not be made responsible for all the differences between one Indo-European dialect and another. It is regrettable that Grumach did not go beyond Anatolia and ponder the linguistic situation in India and Persia. When it is observed that the earliest documents of Indo-Iranian have preserved a linguistic structure fully as copious as that of Homeric Greek and very similar to it in many respects, and furthermore that at least eight centuries must have elapsed between the coming of the Aryans to India and the composition of the *Ṛgveda*, it becomes apparent that Grumach was wrong to deduce a late date for the entry of the Greeks from the character of their earliest literary remains.

About the next part of Grumach's monograph, 'Proximity of the Dialects,' little will be said here, since much of it is concerned with the evidence of Mycenaean Greek. But, Mycenaean apart, we may agree with Grumach that "the Greek dialects are so alike and are so closely interrelated that they cannot have been long separated from one another" (p. 21). It is, indeed, a welcome result of Greek dialect-studies in recent years that greater emphasis is now placed on the similarities between the dialects than on the differences which separate them. But the mere existence of close similarities does nothing to help Grumach's argument, for (so far as the linguistic evidence goes) the various dialect-groups may just as well have lived in close contact within Greece as outside it. Again, it is with some justice that Grumach questions the views of scholars such as Risch and Chadwick, who believe that Doric and Ionic were not formed until after the Dorian migration. But the very argument he deploys against them, namely that it is impossible to date a single one of the linguistic changes they postulate within the history of Greek, undermines his own position as well: if it is true that there is no means whereby any changes can be dated to the Mycenaean age, no more can they be assigned positively to the post-Mycenaean period. The lack of a firmly-based chronology is especially troublesome for Grumach when he discusses the problem of the Ionic dialect. Grumach objects to Chadwick's attempt to date the rise of Ionic after the end of the Mycenaean age; and perhaps he is right to do so, but he needs stronger grounds than are afforded by references in Greek writers to Ionians in the Peloponnese before the Return of the Heraclids. Grumach remarks that it is hard to explain how these references ever originated if there was no basis in fact for the presence of Ionians in such an unexpected area of Greece (p.30). The passage of Herodotus, which is cited as one of the authorities for this statement, is a notoriously obscure one: οἰκέει δὲ τὴν Πελοπόννησον ἔθνεα ἑπτά…οἱ δὲ Κυνούριοι αὐτόχθονες ἐόντες μοῦνοι εἶναι Ἴωνες (8.73). We cannot tell why Herodotus should have regarded the Κυνούριοι as Ionians: that description certainly does not follow (as his words seem to imply) from the mere fact that they are autochthonous. The situation is made more obscure still by the fact that Pausanias regards the Κυνούριοι as Argives of pre-Dorian stock and knows nothing of any Ionian connexion (3.2.2). The suspicion remains that, because earlier in his History (most clearly at 1.56.2) Herodotus has referred to the Ionians as an originally Pelasgian people, so here he makes a simple equation between 'aboriginal' and 'Ionian'. It is true that Pausanias calls the last king of Epidaurus before the Dorian invasion a descendant of Ion (2.26.1) and that Strabo speaks of the early inhabitants of Megara as Ionians (9.1.5). But of what use are such statements to the modern historian? The mention of Megara is irrelevant, while the statements of Herodotus and Pausanias do not appear to rest on any substantial foundation. Even if the ancient writers were correct in locating 'Ionians' in the Peloponnese, they thought of these Ionians as ethnic groups merely, not as speakers of the Ionic dialect; whereas it is the dialect they spoke, and that alone, which would enable us to-day to trace their affinities.[8]

THE HISTORY OF THE DIALECTS

Grumach's belief that the destroyers of the Mycenaean palaces are to be equated with the first Greek arrivals causes him to propound the following account of early migrations and dialect-groupings. The account is based, to a considerable extent, on the

---

[8] It is worth noting that in at least one passage (8.1.2) Strabo confuses ethnic and linguistic divisions.

researches of Porzig.[9] According to Grumach, a three-pronged incursion of Greek-speakers took place at some prehistoric epoch: Ionians moving into central and southern Greece at the same time that 'Aeolo-Achaeans' arrived in Thessaly and Dorians in north-western Greece. Later, Aeolo-Achaeans migrated to the Argolid. Later still, these Aeolo-Achaean settlers were superseded in the Argolid by Dorians, who caused some of them to migrate southward and eastward (p. 35).

Little can be said in favour of these hypotheses. For the three incursions there is no evidence, nor does Grumach claim that there is any. The two linguistic facts he mentions in support of a later migration of Aeolo-Achaeans are exceedingly treacherous and fall far short of establishing a movement of population of the kind and in the direction postulated. (1) The 'Aeolic' substrate in the Peloponnese is a chimera: most of the so-called Aeolic elements which are scattered among the Peloponnesian dialects may be explained as survivals from Common Greek, while the dative plural ending -εσσι could have spread into the Peloponnese in historical times.[10] (2) Grumach sees in the similarity of place-names in the Peloponnese and in Thessaly a further indication that there was a movement of people southward from north-eastern Greece. Long ago, Beloch showed that the

---

[9] *IF* 61 (1954) 147-169.

[10] W. F. Wyatt, *AJPh* 94 (1973) 37-46.

complexities of the Greek migrations in the period before the first Olympiad could not be disentangled by a simple comparison of place-names. While later discoveries have made much of Beloch's argument untenable and changing intellectual fashions have led to a less sceptical reception of legendary accounts, the methodological parts of his paper in which he dissects the evidence for migrations retain much of their value.[11] In the present case, the vital fact we need to know is the epoch at which the transference of place-names from Thessaly to the Peloponnese took place. The similarity of names in itself tells us nothing of this, and to establish an absolute chronology Grumach has recourse (as he must) to the evidence of archaeology. To this we must now turn.

Grumach observes that 'Thessalian' names were attached even to the rivers of Messenia: a fact which, in his belief, proves that the immigration took place at a time when this area was thinly populated, namely in Late Helladic IIIc (p. 36). Furthermore, Grumach follows Milojčić in associating the Dorian invasion of Greece with a second horizon of destruction, to be dated c. 1050 B. C.; subsequently, in the period from the tenth to the eighth century, the Dorians spread over the southern and western parts of the Peloponnese (pp. 37-38). While Grumach may very well be correct in lowering the date at which these parts of Greece received their Dorian colouring, I think that the

---

[11] *RhM* 45 (1890) 555-598.

conclusions he draws from the archaeological evidence are mistaken. The authoritative works of Desborough, Milojčić, and Kimmig (to say nothing of the habits of mind of earlier prehistorians) have taught us to explain the events in Greece at and after the end of the Late Helladic IIIb period in terms of successive invasions from the north and to identify one or other of these invasions with the arrival of Dorian tribes. But now A. M. Snodgrass has cast well justified doubt on the attribution of any decisive change in the culture of Greece at this epoch to northern invaders.[12] To put the matter briefly: despite the superficially impressive assemblages which Milojčić associates with his first and with his second destruction respectively,[13] no single class of object points to an invasion either at the end of Late Helladic IIIb or in Late Helladic IIIc2. The 'violin-bow' fibula, for instance, which makes its first appearance in Greece late in IIIb, has no necessary connection with any northerly region.[14] The flame-shaped spear-head and the Naue II sword, while undoubtedly of European provenience, are represented by good examples in Cyprus at least as early as their occurrence in north-west Greece.[15] This pattern of

---

[12] *PPS* 31 (1965) 229-240; *The dark age of Greece* (Edinburgh 1971) 305-323.

[13] *AA* (1949) 17-18 with fig. 1 and 19-20 with fig. 2.

[14] J. Deshayes, *Argos, les fouilles de la Deiras* (Paris 1966) 208.

[15] H. W. Catling, *Antiquity* 35 (1961) 115-122; *ABSA* 63 (1968) 105-107.

distribution suggests a sporadic and gradual introduction of the new weapon-types into the Mediterranean basin, whether by trade or perhaps by travellers, not the violent replacement of Mycenaean types by northern invaders. With these observations in mind, we may doubt whether there is any support in the archaeological record for Grumach's postulated invasion of Messenia at a time when that part of Greece was sparsely inhabited.

Grumach holds that part of the Achaean population of the Peloponnese was forced to emigrate by the pressure of the Dorian invasion (p. 39). Mainland Greeks are said by Grumach to have settled in two principal areas subsequent to the invasion by the Dorians, namely Cyprus and Crete. In neither of those islands, however, does the course of events really enable us to assert with great confidence that the first settlement by Greeks came after the establishment of the Dorians in the Peloponnese. Different types of evidence are available in each case.

(1) Whether or not Cyprus was colonized by Mycenaeans as early as the thirteenth century B.C. is still an open question. The immense quantities of Mycenaean pottery which have been found not only in coastal regions of Cyprus but also in the interior (as Karageorghis has shown)[16] indicate that there may have been some degree of actual settlement by

---

[16] *Nouveaux documents pour l'étude du Bronze récent à Chypre* (Paris 1965) 137.

Mycenaeans in Late Helladic IIIb.[17] However that may
be, it is true that the first examples of Mycenaean
architecture and metal-working appear at Enkomi after
1200 B. C. But these Mycenaean intrusions cannot
possibly be put as late as Grumach's date of 1050 B. C.
(p. 40): they are dated firmly to the second phase of
the Late Helladic IIIc1 pottery style, c. 1150 B. C.[18] As
for the Aeolic and Ionic elements which are present in
Cypriot but not in Doric, these do not at all lead to the
conclusion, which Grumach regards as inevitable, that
these elements "prevailed amongst the Peloponnesian
population that emigrated to Cyprus" (p. 40): it is
equally likely, or it may be thought more likely, that
Cypriot was contaminated by these Asiatic features
after it had been separated from Arcadian and
established in the eastern Mediterranean.[19]

(2) It is much less easy to follow in detail the
developments in Crete after 1200 B. C, but so far as
our evidence goes at present Grumach is probably
correct in distinguishing two movements from the
Greek mainland, one at the end of Late Helladic IIIb

---

[17] K. Nicolaou, *Acts of the International Archaeological
Symposium 'The Mycenaeans in the Eastern Mediterranean'* (Nicosia
1973) 51-61 would date the first Greek settlements in Cyprus even
earlier in the Mycenaean Age.

[18] Catling, *Cypriot bronze work in the Mycenaean World* (Oxford
1964) 301; A. Furumark, *OpAth* 6 (1965) 99-116; P. Dikaios, *Enkomi
excavations 1948-1958* II (Mainz 1971) 514.

[19] Cf. A. Thumb, *Handbuch der griechischen Dialekte* II (ed. A.
Scherer, Heidelberg 1959) 150.

and the second toward the end of Late Helladic IIIc (p.42). These movements of people may naturally be seen as reactions to the disturbances which affected the Greek mainland, but they do not by themselves tell us anything about the character of the invaders of Greece or confirm the suggestion that there were any invaders.

THE DOMICILE OF THE GREEKS BEFORE THEY ENTERED THE AEGEAN AREA

In the concluding part of his monograph, Grumach brings his hypothesis of a late arrival of the Greeks into connexion with the archaeological and linguistic data. On the archaeological side, he is able to discern one certain fact, namely that at about the end of the thirteenth century B.C. destructive movements of people on a very large scale affected not only Greece but also Anatolia and the Levant. As Grumach sees it, the concept of Greeks, together with other tribes such as Thracians and Illyrians, moving into the Balkans at this time accords well with the archaeological picture of widespread migration (pp. 47-48). Grumach accepts Kimmig's demonstration that the immediate centre of dispersal of the Greeks lay in the Danube basin (pp. 49-50). According to Grumach, the archaeological picture is in harmony with deductions from language. He finds that the eastern Indo-Europeans, including the Greeks, were differentiated from the western groups both negatively and positively: negatively, in that the easterns did not use the term *teuta* 'people' and did not participate in Krahe's system of European hydronymy (p. 51); positively, in that isoglosses between Greek and Armenian show that Greeks and Armenians were living in close contact south-east of the Alps in early times (pp. 52-53). It becomes probable, according to Grumach, that the Armenians migrated from this area as part of the same movement which brought the Greeks southward into Greece (p. 60).

The flaws in the archaeological part of this exposition are perhaps more serious than those in the linguistic part, but a brief examination of both parts is sufficient to show that a migration of Greeks at the time and from the region postulated by Grumach receives no support from any of the types of evidence now available.

To speak first of the archaeological evidence: Grumach has been led astray by the arguments of Kimmig, who sought to account for all the destructive events at the end of the thirteenth century and subsequently by a single far-reaching theory.[20] The concept of vast movements of people from north to south, leaving behind a trail of devastation in Greece and the eastern Mediterranean, has proved a seductive one, especially because it seemed to be consistent with the Egyptian records of the Sea Raiders and to account for the overthrow of such powerful kingdoms as those of the Hittites, the Syrians, and the Mycenaeans. It is

---

[20] W. Kimmig, *Studien aus Alteuropa* I (ed. Uslar, Cologne 1964) 220-283.

very doubtful whether this explanation holds good even in the east, where the collapse of the Hittite empire is more plausibly to be attributed to economic causes, the destruction of Ugarit to the effects of an earthquake,[21] and the formidable effects of the Sea Raiders' incursions to exaggeration by Egyptian scribes.[22] So far as the Aegean is concerned, there remains one great obstacle in the way of those who wish to ascribe the disasters to foreign invaders: Namely that the material culture of mainland Greece continues to be Mycenaean, above all in respect of pottery.[23] The changes which occur in the material culture of Greece just after 1200 B. C. consist of the abandonment of certain Mycenaean habits, such as building in stone and the construction of tholos-tombs, not in the wholesale submergence of these habits by foreign customs. In Greece, as well as in the eastern Mediterranean, the archaeological record simply does not yield a series of objects which were introduced at the same time and which can be associated with a specific culture to the north.

Grumach's observations that the east Indo-Europeans did not use the western term *teuta* remains broadly true, although some scattered occurrences of

---

[21] C.F.-A. Schaeffer, *Ugaritica* V (Paris 1968) 754-768.

[22] S. Donadoni, *RSI* 77 (1965) 300-314.

[23] Furumark, *OA* 3 (1944) 194-265. The evidence cited by J. B. Rutter, *AJA* (1975) 17-31 is of extreme interest, but it does not suffice to alter the general picture in any important respect.

this word have now been found in the eastern regions as well.[24] Nor is it possible to deny that some of the isoglosses shared by Greek and Armenian strongly suggest that speakers of these languages lived in contiguity for a long period after they had been split off from Indo-European: the most significant isoglosses are found in morphological features such as augment, genitive singular in *-osyo*, and 'prothetic' vowel, and in the items of vocabulary listed by Porzig.[25] But, while these linguistic facts enable us to surmise with reasonable confidence that proto-Greeks and proto-Armenians were neighbors, they do not permit us to say what part of the world the two peoples inhabited or to what epoch their co-existence belonged. It is vital to Grumach's case that the chronological limits at least should be fixed; but all that can be said about the lower limit is that "it is now generally acknowledged that about 1200 B. C. the ancestors of the Armenians moved out of the Balkans into Anatolia and remained for a long period in central and northern Anatolia in the old Hittite linguistic area" (p. 58). A migration of proto-Armenians into Anatolia at the time of the dissolution of the Hittite empire undoubtedly fits neatly into what is known of the

---

[24] Scherer, *Kratylos* 10 (1965) 19.

[25] *Die Gliederung des indogermanischen Sprachgebiets* (Heidelberg 1954) 155-157 (cited by Grumach). Resemblances which have been claimed to exist between Greek and Armenian in the field of phonology are less easy to substantiate: note the doubts expressed by Szemerényi, *SMEA* 1 (1966) 38-39.

history of the area; but positive facts in support of an Armenian migration are lacking. The Armeno-Hittite isoglosses cited by Grumach at p. 59 are certainly consistent with the picture he is constructing; but they in no way impose belief in the correctness of this picture. Suppose that the proto-Armenians did indeed live close to the proto-Greeks in the Danube basin, and suppose further that the proto-Armenians did move out of this region c.1200 B. C.: what would these facts, if they could be established, prove about the movements of the proto-Greeks? Obviously nothing, in spite of Grumach's implicit assumption that the two peoples must have moved out of their homeland at about the same time, on their way to help destroy respectively the Mycenaean and the Hittite kingdoms. But, simply because these peoples are known to have shared some important linguistic features, we are not entitled to infer that the course of their history followed parallel lines. No linguistic or historical fact exists which would prevent our forming a rival hypothesis, according to which groups of Greek-speakers periodically detached themselves from the main area of Greek speech (whatever that was) and made their way into Greece; and none of Grumach's arguments proves that this could not have been an immensely long process, which perhaps began as early as the Middle Helladic period and which may not have been completed until late in the Bronze Age.

CONCLUSIONS

Now that the principal heads of Grumach's argument have been reviewed, a further, important matter bearing on the date of the Greeks' arrival remains to be discussed, even though it is not mentioned by Grumach himself. Leaving aside the question whether or not the Greek language is represented in the monuments of Bronze Age Greece, we cannot avoid reference to the preservation, in Greek literature and tradition, of direct memories of Bronze Age Greece. As the details are so well known, the briefest description of these memories will suffice here; but it will be necessary to consider at greater length the implications for the present argument. Greek memories of the Bronze Age fall into two main classes. (1) The configuration and order of importance of the sites described in the Catalogue of Ships correspond to the state of affairs which is known to have existed in the Mycenaean age but not at any subsequent period,[26] while Homeric descriptions of actual Bronze Age objects (for example the silver-studded sword, the bronze corslet, the boar's tusk helmet, and the body-shield of Ajax) can have originated only in the Bronze Age.[27] (2) Since cycles of legend are so frequently associated with Mycenaean

---

[26] D.L. Page, *History and the Homeric Iliad* (Berkeley and Los Angeles 1959) 118-124; R. Hope Simpson and J. F. Lazenby, *The Catalogue of the Ships in Homer's Iliad* (Oxford 1970) 153-175.

[27] G.S. Kirk, *The songs of Homer* (Cambridge 1962) 181-182.

centres (centres, again, which were sometimes of no consequence whatever after the end of the Bronze Age), we may infer with a high degree of confidence that the legends themselves arose in the Mycenaean period.[28]

How the proponent of a late date for the arrival of the Greeks is to behave in the face of these facts, I do not know for certain; but it seems to me that the only way of saving the hypothesis would be to argue that the Greek immigrants assimilated the legends and narrative traditions of the Mycenaeans so completely that by the time that the Homeric poems were composed it is no longer possible to distinguish the 'Mycenaean' from the 'Greek' strain. It is by no means incredible, in theory, that one people could absorb the culture of another to such an extent as to result in the amalgam seen in the *Iliad* and *Odyssey*. However, I do not think it would be open to Grumach and his school to argue that this was the actual course of events in Greece during the Late Bronze Age and the early part of the Iron Age. Although Grumach provides so little detail about the supersession of 'Mycenaean' by 'Greek' that it is very difficult to visualize exactly what kind of process he has in mind, it is worth recalling an expression used at an earlier stage of his monograph: "the Greeks migrated *against the trend of*

---

[28] M.P. Nilsson, *ANTIΔΩPON Festschrift J. Wachernagel* (Göttingen 1923) 137-142; *The Mycenaean origin of Greek mythology* (Berkeley and Los Angeles 1932) 27-28.

civilization.... They were half-civilized migrants who burst into an area of comparatively advanced civilization" (p. 12).

But the concept of "half-civilized" Greeks who invaded the Mycenaean area and destroyed many settlements of the Mycenaeans is so much at variance with the observed facts of the Greek traditions as absolutely to be excluded by them. One people could have taken over the culture of another to the extent attested in one of two ways: either the newcomers lived in harmony with at least part of the native population for a long period; or the newcomers enjoyed such a cultural ascendancy that they were able, quickly and easily, to absorb the skills and traditions of the natives. The overwhelming difficulty inherent in Grumach's hypothesis is that neither of these alternatives can obtain. So far from thinking of a period of peaceful co-existence between invaders and aborigines, Grumach postulates a violent irruption accompanied by destruction of sites, thereby leaving no time for traditions to be transferred from one people to the other; but, on the other hand, the newcomers are only "half-civilized migrants," who would have needed a great length of time even to adapt to the new conditions of life in Greece, still more, to take over, and use as their own, the descriptions of Mycenaean Greece and of Mycenaean artefacts which must already have been expressed in literary form.

I believe that grave doubt is cast upon Grumach's thesis by the considerations offered in earlier parts of this paper but that the arguments from Homer and the Greek traditions make that thesis completely incredible. It is very much to be hoped that, if a historian subsequently tries to argue along the same lines as those followed in Grumach's monograph, he will direct his attention particularly to the resolution of this difficulty, which at present seems to me fatal to the whole case for a late arrival of Greek-speakers.

APPENDIX

There follows a list of words cited by Grumach as evidence of intrusion by Greeks at a late date. Each word is attested first in the source given in brackets.

ἄμβιξ (Athenaeus)

Origin completely obscure. The - ιξ seems to be secondary, by analogy with κύλιξ; if so, ἄμβ- is the same stem which appears in ἄμβη and ἄμβων.

ἄναξ (*Iliad*)

J. Puhvel suggests the unconvincing Indo-European derivation *wṇn-ṇk-(t)* 'not subject to doom', *ZVS* 73 (1956) 202-222. C.J. Ruijgh, *Lingua* 25 (1970) 309-312 regards it as a loan-word.

ἀρύβαλλος (Stesichorus)

Probably a purely Greek compound, ἀρύ- ω + βάλλ- ω : Ernst Fraenkel, *Glotta* 4 (1913) 35. For a different view, but still taking Greek as the starting-point, see O. Haas, *WS* 71(1958) 166 n. 20.

βασιλεύς (Iliad)

Disputed. There is no reason to think it belongs to a

Mediterranean substrate. An Indo-European derivation was proposed by A. Bezzenberger, *BB* 3 (1879) 174 and O.Wiedemann, *ZVS* 33 (1895) 163-164 who associate βασι- with Lithuanian *giñti* and regard the -λο- as a diminutive suffix. Szemérnyi, ΜΝΗΜΗΣ ΧΑΡΙΝ II (Vienna 1957) 177 n. 59 regards βασιλεύς as a loan from an Asianic language (*pati-lo* from an Indo-European *poti-*). A. Heubeck, *IF* 63 (1958) 134-135 sees βασιλεύς as a lengthened form in -*l*- from a word *βάσις meaning 'tribe, family.'

βῖκος (Hipponax)

G. Nencioni, *SIFC* 16 (1939) 223-226 showed that βῖκος was unlikely to belong to a Mediterranean substrate. Émilia Masson, *Recherches sur le plus anciens emprunts sémitiques mitiques en Grec* (Paris 1967) 78-80 regards it as a possible, but not certain, loan from a Semitic source. It is perhaps a loan from Egyptian according to B. Hemmerdinger, *Glotta* 48 (1970) 54-55.

βλῆτρον (*Iliad*)

There is no reason not to connect this word with βάλλω, P. Chantraine, *Dictionnaire étymologique de la langue grecque* (Paris 1968) s.v.

γεῖσον (Euripides)

Quite apart from its late appearance, there is nothing to connect γεῖσον with a Mediterranean substrate. Steph. Byz. s.v. Μονόγισ(σ)α calls it a Carian word corresponding to Greek λίθος (Μονόγισσα = Μονόλιθος).

γέφυρα (*Iliad*)

Obscure. A. Meillet's attempt to connect it with Armenian *kamurj BSL* 22 (1920) 17 appears to fail on phonetic grounds; but Kretschmer suggested that the dialectal differences found within Greek pointed to an Indo-European origin of some kind, *Glotta* 22 (1934) 259.

δέπας (*Iliad*)

Probably cognate with Hieroglyphic Hittite *tapas-/tepas-* 'cup' as suggested by E. Laroche, *Les hiéroglyphes hittites* I (Paris 1960) 96. V. Pisani sees a connexion with Hittite *tapisana-*, *Lingue e culture* (Brescia 1969) 194-196.

δοῦλος (δούλη in *Iliad*)

Dubious. It was explained as a loan from south-west Anatolia through the medium of Ionic by M. Lambertz, *Glotta* 4 (1915) 1-18. Heubeck, *IF* 63 (1958) 134 n. 102 and *Lydiaka* (Erlangen 1959) 69 regards it as an *-l-* formation of Lydian type (*δοσε-λος). It is associated with an Indo-European stem *dema-* 'build, tame' by A. Tovar, *Acta Mycenaea* II (Salamanca 1972) 318-325.

εἰρήνη (*Iliad*)

No secure etymology.

ἑρμηνεύς (Pindar)

A borrowing from Semitic *targumānu*, according to Szemérnyi, *Gnomon* 43 (1971) 668.

θριγκός (*Odyssey*)

No secure etymology.

καμάρα (Herodotus)

A loan from Iranian. Avestan *kamarā-* 'belt' satisfactorily accounts for, even if it does not explain, Hesychius' gloss καμάριαι· ζῶναι στρατιωτικαί.

κάμινος ('Homeric' epigram)

No secure etymology.

κάνθαρος (Aristophanes)

The presence of -νθ- has inevitably provoked the suggestion of 'Pelasgian' or 'Mediterranean' etymologies: cf. L. Gil Fernández, *Nombres de insectos en Griego antiguo* (Madrid 1959) 226-228. But its evidence is of little value to those who are constructing theories about cultural or linguistic strata, since it is doubtful whether the word originally denoted a vessel at all. The fact that it means also 'dung-beetle' suggests that it may have been used only secondarily of a vessel shaped like a beetle. On the other hand, Szemérnyi, *Gnomon* 43 (1971) 672 sees the word as a loan from Akkadian *kandaru* 'kind of vessel'.

κελέβη (Anacreon)

No secure etymology.

κέραμος (*Iliad*)

No secure etymology.

κισσύβιον (*Odyssey*)

The ending is difficult, but if the word is associated with κισσός, that at least can be given an Indo-

European derivation: H. Petersson, *IF* 24 (1909) 252.

κώθων (Archilochus)

No secure etymology.

λαός (*Iliad*)

Dubious. Heubeck, *Studi linguistici in onore di Vittore Pisani* II (Brescia 1969) 543-544 sees a connexion with Hittite *laḫḫa-*.

λήκυθος (*Odyssey*)

Dubious. The connexion with Lithuanian *lenkti* is regarded as too risky by Eduard Hermann, *Glotta* 13 (1923) 152 (in any case, the ending -υθος still has to be explained): he prefers to see it as a loan-word. L.J. Elferink, *Lekythos* (Amsterdam 1934) 21-48 tried to associate λήκυθος and λέκιθος with κύτος, but this theory has rightly found little favour.

μέγαρον (*Iliad*)

Obscure. Could there be a connexion with μέγας? At least this seems more likely than the derivation suggested by L. Deroy, *RBPh* 26 (1948) 526-527 (Sanskrit *āgāra*). Cf. Masson, *Emprunts* 87-88 for the possibility of a loan from Semitic.

ὀπυίω (*Iliad*)

M. Hammerström, *Glotta* 11 (1921) 212 supports the connexion with Etruscan *puia*; despite the difficulties, which Hammerström himself mentions, nothing more plausible has so far been suggested. Less convincingly, J. Wackernagel saw a connexion with Sanskrit *puṣyati*: *Sprachliche Untersuchungen zu Homer* (Göttingen 1916) 228 n. 1.

πλίνθος (Herodotus)

Both Indo-European and non-Indo-European derivations have been proposed: see the discussion by G. Alessio, *SE* 18 (1944) 139-141. The word is best regarded as a loan from Semitic: Szemérnyi, *JHS* 94 (1974) 149.

πρεσβευτής (Thucydides)

Ernst Fraenkel, *Glotta* 32 (1953) 17 sees a connexion with Sanskrit *purogava-*.

πρύτανις (proper name in *Iliad*)

This word is seen as a loan from Asia Minor by Heubeck, *Praegraeca* (Erlangen 1961) 67-68 and Szemérnyi, *JHS* 94 (1974) 154.

πύργος (*Iliad*)

This too is regarded by Heubeck as a loan from Anatolia: *Praegraeca* 63-65.

τύραννος (Alcaeus)

A connexion with Hieroglyphic Hittite *tarwana-* is probable: Laroche, *Hiér. hitt.* 197-198; Heubeck, *Praegraeca* 68-70; R. Gusmani, *Studi Pisani* I 511-512.

φιάλη (*Iliad*)

No secure etymology.

II

THE COMING OF THE GREEKS—II

When, and in what circumstances, did the first Greek-speakers enter Greece? Such questions I pondered in 'The coming of the Greeks', *Historia* 25 (1976), 129-145. The 1976 paper was written in response to the speculations of my late friend Ernst Grumach, who had dated the arrival of Greek-speakers to a time after the collapse of the Mycenaean palatial system. The date proposed by Grumach was consistent with the belief that the Linear B documents of the Aegean Bronze Age did not contain Greek. Although this belief was not then, and is not now, widely shared, I thought that Grumach's arguments were sufficiently interesting to be examined on their own merits, irrespective of the presence of Greek in the Linear B archives. By considering one by one the items of vocabulary adduced by Grumach, I tried to show that some at least of these could not have come into use in Greece as late as the first millennium B.C.

Although I have no doubt that Greek was spoken and written on the mainland and in Crete much earlier than Grumach was willing to concede, I remain uncertain how far back the history of Greek can in fact be traced. If a *communis opinio* can be said to exist, it is to the effect that a recognizable 'Greek language' was in existence by about 1900 B.C. But about its origin there appears to be no agreement: some believing that a form of Greek was introduced from outside by Indo-European immigrants, others that immigrants formed the Greek language after their arrival, by combining their own Indo-European speech with the indigenous language (or languages). The proponents of each view naturally think of an incursion into Greece by a specific group at a specific time.

Many enquirers in the past thought it permissible to define both the group and the time. They equated the intrusive group with invaders who entered Greece early in the second millennium B.C. and introduced the material culture known conventionally as 'Middle Helladic'.[1] More than one attitude may be adopted towards equations of this kind. Either they are ruled out altogether, on the ground that there is never any necessary correlation between linguistic changes and changes in the material record. Or such an equation may have potential value, provided that the material changes are such as to impose belief in a change of population and the introduction of a new language.

By the thirties of the present century the main characteristics both of Early Helladic and of the

---

[1] So, for example, J.B. Haley and C.W. Blegen, *AJA* 32 (1928), 141-154.

succeeding Middle Helladic were well understood. It was clear also that most of the known Early Helladic sites had been destroyed, more or less violently. Such were:

- Boeotia: Eutresis, Orchomenos.

- Attica: Ayios Kosmas.

- Corinthia and Argolis: Asine, Korakou, Tiryns, Zygouries.

- Arcadia: Asea.

- Messenia: Malthi.

After their destruction, most of these sites were re-occupied; but the material culture of their inhabitants in the Middle Helladic age was, by and large, appreciably different from, and poorer than, the preceding Early Helladic culture. The hall-marks of Middle Helladic include house-plans of a simple rectangular or apsidal type, burial in cist-graves, and the pottery-styles known as 'Minyan' and 'matt-painted'. It is, however, not easy to point to a given place in central or southern Greece and say, 'here the Middle Helladic invaders entered Greece, destroying the Early Helladic sites and re-settling the country'. For although several Early Helladic sites were devastated, there is lacking from the record a 'horizon of destruction' which would mark the definitive end of an entire way of life. Nor (a point not always fully appreciated) is there any reason to identify the destroyers of the Early Helladic sites with the new Middle Helladic people. It is possible, for example, that the Early Helladic sites fell in the course of internecine warfare (which would be consistent with the powerful fortifications found at some settlements), and the intruders entered Greece as the beneficiaries, but not the agents, of destruction. Nevertheless it seemed certain that, whatever the precise rôle of the Middle Helladic people, *they must have entered Greece from outside* and could thus be identified, at least *prima facie*, as the bearers of Indo-European speech. The postulate of an intrusion was, apparently, well founded; and the profound changes attendant on the intrusion sufficed to attest the arrival of a new people and a new language.

So matters stood in 1950. In the ensuing decade excavations were conducted at Lerna in Argolis, which turned out to be richer in Early Helladic material than any other known site. The excavations also pointed to a sequence of events which seemed to contradict the evidence of other places inhabited both in Early and in Middle Helladic. Lerna was destroyed not at the end, but in the course, of the Early Helladic period; 'Lerna IV' was a new settlement founded after the destruction, and in time it developed without a further break into the Middle Helladic town known as 'Lerna V'. Not only that, but a type of pottery closely akin to Grey Minyan was produced in Lerna IV, which in other respects seemed to be a typical Early Helladic settlement. So it appeared that, at least at Lerna, the 'Middle Helladic people' were responsible neither for the destruction nor for the introduction of Grey

Minyan ware. The destruction had to be attributed to some other, unknown, cause; while the Grey Minyan ware was shown to have no necessary connexion with the Middle Helladic people but to be the result of indigenous development.

When Caskey presented these facts in a lucid paper,[2] he tried to bring the other Early Helladic sites into harmony with Lerna. After re-examining the reports, he suggested that the following sites were destroyed at about the same time as Lerna (namely at the end of Early Helladic II, not the end of Early Helladic III): Asine, Ayios Kosmas, Tiryns, Zygouries. The material from Korakou did not allow a final decision to be made. Only at Eutresis did Caskey concede a destruction at the end of the Early Helladic period.

Caskey therefore showed that the appearance of the Middle Helladic culture was not at Lerna, and perhaps not elsewhere, accompanied either by devastation or by intrusive elements (of which Minyan ware was the most distinctive). Despite his demonstration that no feature typical of Middle Helladic could be shown to have been introduced from outside, Caskey was convinced that there had been widespread devastation by foreign invaders; but this devastation had occurred between the second and third phases of Early Helladic, not at the end of Early Helladic III. The Middle Helladic people too he thought were probably

---

[2] J.L. Caskey, *Hesperia* 29 (1960), 285-303.

foreigners, but foreigners who peacefully assumed control of several settlements. Caskey saw no reason to dissent from the prevailing view that the Middle Helladic people were the ancestors of the Mycenaeans, and so of the later Greeks; his modification consisted in seeing some degree of kinship between the Middle Helladic people and the people of Early Helladic III. Caskey thus shifted the archaeological ground for the incursion of Greek-speakers, but by no means removed it altogether.

Recent excavations in the lower citadel at Tiryns corroborate Caskey's results in one respect, but in another suggest that events took a different course from that at Lerna. At Tiryns, as at Lerna, a type of Minyan ware made its appearance in the Early Helladic levels.[3] There was not, however, that decisive break between Early Helladic II and III which Caskey detected at Lerna; on the contrary, there was a 'transitional horizon' (early phase of Early Helladic III), in which Early Helladic II elements persisted.[4] In whatever way the chronology of Tiryns is to be reconciled with that of Lerna, it seems evident that we should no longer accept Caskey's hypothesis of a general destruction affecting the Argolid sites at the end of Early Helladic II. Since, on Caskey's own

---

[3] H.-J. Weisshaar, *AA* (1981), 246.

[4] Weisshaar, *AA* (1982), 462-463. No certain evidence of a 'transitional horizon' has yet been found at other Argolid sites: cf. D.J. Pullen, *AJA* 91 (1987), 533-544.

showing, there was no widespread devastation at the end of Early Helladic III, and no evidence that any significant elements of material culture were introduced from outside, the old equation of Middle Helladic invaders with the first Greek-speakers has been completely discredited.

Is the arrival of Greek-speakers, then, to be dissociated completely from changes and developments in the material record? Should we not rather think of a gradual assimilation of Indo-European-speakers with the speakers of indigenous languages? Such an assimilation may have taken a very long time to run its course, but was in any case complete (at latest) by the fifteenth century B.C.[5]

Many modern writers on these topics believe, no doubt rightly, that the arrival of Greek-speakers raises a question which must be considered in the context of the 'Indo-European problem' as a whole. This problem in effect resolves itself into three: the location of the Indo-European homeland, the manner in which the Indo-European-speakers dispersed, and the time of their dispersal.

To these vast questions various answers have been given, depending on different interpretations of the linguistic evidence. From a superficial point of view, it is an easy matter to arrive at the underlying lexicon

---

[5] It is obvious that a lapse of time (of unknown duration) must be allowed between the creation of the Linear B script and the date of the extant inscriptions: cf. M. Lejeune, *BSL* 71 (1976), 195.

common to the Indo-European people prior to their dispersal, then to predict the type of material culture which would have marked the Indo-Europeans, and finally to match this culture with one actually attested in the archaeological record. But neither the assumption nor the method is acceptable. The assumption is false, since to construct a 'protolexicon' of Indo-European takes insufficient account of linguistic, and especially semantic, change: it is one thing to extract a basic vocabulary which might be thought common to the Indo-Europeans before their migrations; quite another to be sure that the items of this vocabulary had the same meaning throughout the 'Indo-European era' that they bore in the historical languages. But, even if these objections could be overcome, a set of lexical terms (which is a pure abstraction) cannot be transferred bodily to a particular culture whose attributes are known only through the medium of archaeology. Some artefacts, some animals, some trees named in the protolexicon will be present in a given culture, but some will not. A satisfactory marriage between the linguistic and the archaeological data, even of a crude kind, will never be achieved.

Suppose it could be shown (in spite of these reservations) that a people of relatively homogeneous culture, possessing at least some of the properties indicated by the protolexicon, had in the course of its migrations a decisive impact upon other populations: could not that people be identified as 'Indo-European' and its migrations equated with the Indo-European dispersal? Affirmative answers have been returned by Marija Gimbutas, who makes such a claim for the 'Kurgan' culture of the south Russian steppe:

> Constantly accumulating archaeological discoveries have effectively eliminated the earlier theories of Indo-European homelands in central or northern Europe and in the Balkans. The Kurgan culture seems the only remaining candidate for being Proto-Indo-European: there was no other culture in the Neolithic and Chalcolithic periods which would correspond with the hypothetical mother culture of the Indo-Europeans as reconstructed with the help of common words, and there were no other great expansions and conquests affecting whole territories where earliest historic sources and a cultural continuum prove the existence of Indo-European speakers.[6]

In this and later publications Marija Gimbutas has spoken of successive waves of Kurgan expansion into Europe, which she traces on the map: these waves she identifies as the migrations of the Indo-European people. From the archaeological point of view, the synthesis is an impressive one, since it takes account of, and offers an explanation for, observed changes in the material culture of central and eastern Europe. And at least one prominent Indo-Europeanist has embraced the synthesis without much reservation, namely André Martinet in his book *Des Steppes aux Océans* (Paris

---

[6] *Indo-European and Indo-Europeans* (ed. G. Cardona, H.M. Hoenigswald, A. Senn) (Philadelphia 1970), 155-197 (p. 156).

1987). Despite this impressive endorsement, I cannot regard the Kurgan hypothesis as an answer to the Indo-European problem in general or to the Greek problem in particular.

Looking first at the Indo-European problem, we observe that the answer proposed is, at best, only a partial one. Much is said, and well said, about the cultural changes in Europe, especially those of the fourth and third millennia B.C. Even with regard to these regions, there is no attempt to relate the changes in material culture to the emergence of the languages actually attested in historical times. But (and this is a more serious shortcoming) the eastern Indo-European-speakers find no place in the account. Who, then, were the Indo-European migrants to India and Persia? No evidence, so far as I know, indicates that they were Kurgan people. But, if they were not, it follows that an Indo-European migration has no necessary connexion with a movement of the Kurgan people; and in Europe too, even if the Kurgan people were responsible for all the material changes attributed to them, not a single one of these changes can be associated positively with Indo-Europeans *qua* Indo-Europeans.

Nor has the Kurgan hypothesis any decisive hearing upon the arrival of Indo-European-speakers in Greece. Mention is certainly made of the destruction of Argolid sites at the end of Early Hellenic II,[7] but the succeeding culture has little in common with that of

---

[7] *Op. cit.*, p. 186.

the 'Kurgan people', and, as already demonstrated, it turns out that there was no widespread and co-ordinated devastation in Greece during the third millennium—certainly none that we have any right to associate with the incursion of a new linguistic group.

Such, in exceedingly brief outline, are the immediate antecedents of Colin Renfrew's *Archaeology and Language* (London 1987), in which the brilliant author discusses both the Indo-European problem and the arrival of Greek-speakers. Several received opinions fall like ninepins before Renfrew's trenchant argument. First there is the notion that languages are introduced into a given region only as the result of migrations or invasions. As Renfrew makes plain, this assumption has no basis in fact or even probability; it is closely connected with another assumption, no less erroneous, that far-reaching changes in the material record inevitably point to linguistic changes. The validity of a 'protolexicon' as an infallible means of ascertaining the Indo-European homeland is briskly, and quite properly, dismissed. The entire edifice of 'glottochronology' is dismantled, as not providing even the reliable 'chronological' answer claimed for it. Finally, Renfrew robustly denies that a valid comparison can be made between the mythology, legal system, and social organization of one Indo-European people and another. Here I feel that Renfrew may go too far, because (as will presently emerge) I differ from him with respect to the date of the dispersal; at the same time, I think he is successful in exposing as fallacious Dumézil's concept of a tripartite social system peculiar to the Indo-Europeans.

Renfrew's reluctance to accept invasions and migrations as explaining the Indo-European dispersal (a reluctance I share) leads him to make radically new proposals. He places the original homeland in eastern Anatolia, from which (he believes) Indo-European languages (or, perhaps, an undifferentiated language) were carried gradually westwards with the spread of the earliest farmers. Since these farmers are known, on the basis of radio-carbon dates, to have reached Greece and Crete by the end of the seventh millennium B.C., their departure from the homeland must have occurred at a much earlier period. Renfrew thus replaces the established 'model of élite dominance' (whereby a new people at a high cultural level imposes its language upon the natives) by the 'wave of advance model', that is to say the gradual diffusion of a language through contact between human communities.

Renfrew has done much to make implausible the equation which used to be drawn between linguistic change and the wholesale movements of peoples. In particular, he has provided reasons (in addition to those advanced above) for dissociating the upheavals of Early Bronze Age Greece from the rise of the Greek language. But the positive proposals made in *Archaeology and Language* are no more acceptable than the theories so elegantly, and so cogently, refuted there. The remainder of this short paper will be devoted to a critique of these proposals, in the hope that a more satisfactory synthesis of views can be achieved.

From a specifically 'Greek' view-point, I may perhaps raise two questions in respect of Renfrew's book. The first question is one of method: does Renfrew adopt a sound procedure for identifying the Indo-European homeland and describing the manner in which Indo-Europeans migrated from their homeland? The second concerns the properties of the Greek language itself and its relationships with other Indo-European languages: are these adequately explained by Renfrew?

The first, or methodological, question concerns three matters above all: homeland, migrations, 'models'.

With regard to the *homeland*, preference has been given to one or another region because it seemed well suited as a starting-point for the Indo-European migrations—or, sometimes, because it was felt appropriate to a conquering 'Aryan' race. Although any location of the homeland based on purely 'racial' grounds is now (I hope universally) repudiated, valid criteria for identifying the homeland are much harder to establish. Renfrew rejects the answers given by the protolexicon, and he is right to do so. But what approach is left? It is at this stage that I believe Renfrew goes astray in his turn. For, so far as I can see, there is only one good reason for his placing the homeland in eastern Anatolia: namely that there the existence of farming communities is first attested. But who would confidently identify the earliest farming folk with proto-Indo-Europeans? Only (I believe) those who had already persuaded themselves that the westward migration of Indo-Europeans was in some way connected with the diffusion of an economy based on farming. Such a method of discovering the homeland is no more commendable than those rejected by Renfrew, since they at least took some account of the linguistic data, however fragmentary and poorly understood those data may have been.

The westward *migrations* are seen by Renfrew as a process, not a series of aggressive incursions. Since we are completely ignorant of the precise manner in which Indo-European languages became established over such a vast area, Renfrew's explanation is as likely as the other. It would become more likely only if there were some positive means of identifying the first farmers as the bearers of Indo-European speech. But we have no such means. When Renfrew (rightly, in my view) refuses to regard as Indo-Europeans a specific people leaving traces in the archaeological record, he should be equally sceptical of the earliest farming communities in Greece, for these too exist for us only in so far as they can be defined in archaeological terms: about their language we know no more than we know about the speech of the 'Early Helladic folk' or the 'Middle Helladic folk' or the kings buried in the Shaft Graves. That they practised farming indeed marks a decisive advance over their predecessors; but it is an advance which has meaning in cultural, not in linguistic, terms—and Renfrew (again rightly) has insisted on the necessity of regarding 'Indo-Europeans' solely in the light of their linguistic affinities.

The justification for Renfrew's *model* lies in the fact that, in very broad terms, the spread of farming can be traced in a westerly direction. But what of the east? There is no evidence of the gradual adoption of farming from west to east, that might be correlated with the European pattern. Hence Renfrew is driven to ponder a choice between alternative hypotheses: either (despite the lack of evidence) the process was, after all, similar to that attested for Europe or a more complex sequence of events has to be envisaged, with a wave of farmers succeeded by nomad pastoralists, groups of whom imposed themselves according to the model of 'élite dominance'. I am not aware that these nomads or élites have any existence outside the realm of theory: none, certainly, that can be connected plausibly with the diffusion of Indo-European speech. But in the real world (as Renfrew acknowledges) there is one cultural phenomenon that makes its appearance at about the same time in India and in the lands bordering the Aegean Sea. This phenomenon concerns the use of the draught-horse and, in particular, of the horse-drawn chariot. Naturally there is no place in Renfrew's scheme for the old view that horses and chariots are indisputable marks of a conquering 'Aryan' or 'Indo-European' folk. And it is true that no positive case has even been made out for the exclusively 'Indo-European' character of horses or chariots. To Renfrew

the use of the equipage presents no problem. He
regards it as a development occurring independently in
India and the Aegean, at a time when both those
regions had long been settled by people of Indo-
European speech. But, at least so far as the Aegean is
concerned, this hypothesis involves an over-
simplification, perhaps an outright distortion, of the
evidence. The areas in which the use of the chariot is
attested as early as the sixteenth and fifteenth centuries
B.C., namely the Argolid plain and the environs of
Knossos,[8] offer a terrain very poorly suited to chariot-
driving. This circumstance makes it unlikely that the
practice of driving chariots was called into being by
purely local conditions; it was, no doubt, introduced
from elsewhere.[9] Only a 'military élite' would have felt
the need of possessing chariots, whether for service or
for conspicuous display. I mention these points, not
because I believe they have any direct bearing upon
the Indo-European question, but in order to show how
easy it is to manipulate 'models': these should be
confined, as a matter of principle, to the archaeological

---

[8]   To the information set out in Evans' *PM* IV, 826-832, add S.
Alexiou, *AA* (1964), 785-804 and M.A.S. Cameron, *AA* (1967), 330-
344. It is not certain whether the chariot-scenes on the Shaft Grave
stelae depict warfare or hunting: cf. G.E. Mylonas, *AJA* 55 (1951),
134-147. The *i-qi-ja* of the Knossos tablets, however, are plainly war-
chariots. On the whole question, M.A. Littauer, *AJA* 76 (1972), 145-
157.

[9]   F. Schachermeyr set out the relevant facts at *Anthropos* 46
(1951), 705-753, but was (I believe) mistaken in thinking that the
Mycenaeans had learnt the use of the chariot in Egypt.

domain and not applied to the solution of linguistic problems.

From general questions of method I turn to the Greek language itself. Two matters are of special interest here: substrate and the relations of Greek with other Indo-European languages.

That there was a non-Greek *substrate* which left numerous unassimilated traces in Greek words is acknowledged by Renfrew (pp. 176-177). Such traces are of various kinds, but here I consider only the -σ(σ)- and -νθ- formants found in the names of rivers, mountains, plants, and settlements: Πήδασος, Κηφισός, Παρνασσός, ὑάκινθος, Κόρινθος, Κνωσός, and many others. For a long time, quite naturally, these -σ(σ)- and -νθ- elements were regarded as the relics not only of a non-Greek, but of a non-Indo-European, language. The non-Indo-European character of such elements seemed assured by the parallels to which Kretschmer gave classic expression. Corresponding to the Greek words with -νθ- and -σ(σ)- were a series of Anatolian toponyms containing the -nd- or the -ss- element. But the languages spoken in Asia Minor prior to the Greek colonization were thought to be pre-Indo-European. For these reasons Kretschmer postulated a linguistic community embracing both Anatolia and the Aegean region: this community (he thought) was in time disrupted by the arrival in Greece of the first Greek-speakers, who incorporated into their language elements of the substrate.[10] The later discovery that Indo-European languages, for instance Hittite and Luwian, had been spoken in Anatolia during the Bronze Age led Kretschmer to revise his conclusion fundamentally. It had become obvious that some place-names, and other words, in these languages contained *-ss-* and *-nd-* elements, directly comparable with the pre-Greek $-\sigma(\sigma)-$ and $-\nu\theta-$; to take account of this new evidence, Kretschmer reckoned with a 'proto-Indo-European stratum', common to Anatolia and the Aegean, which he dated to the time of the Minoan palaces. This was succeeded by an 'Indo-European stratum', marked by the arrival of Greek-speaking immigrants.[11] This argument was accepted by a later generation of scholars, who however modified it in one important respect. It has been established since Kretschmer's time that there is nothing 'primitive' about Hittite or Luwian and that these languages cannot be assigned (as Kretschmer thought) to a 'proto-Indo-European' stage. The modern view is that the *-nd-*/$-\nu\theta-$ and *-ss-*/$-\sigma\sigma-$ equations attest the presence in Anatolia of languages with 'Indo-European' credentials no less sound than those of Greek itself;[12] in other words, that

---

[10] P. Kretschmer, *Einleitung in die Geschichte der griechischen Sprache* (Göttingen 1896), 293-322, 402-408.

[11] Id., *Glotta* 14 (1925), 312-319. Kretschmer later drew a more detailed comparison between the Aegean and the Anatolian toponyms: *Glotta* 28 (1940), 234-255.

[12] E. Laroche, *RHA* 69 (1961), 91. It is possible, but not certain, that a similar situation obtained in Europe. Hans Krahe was

words, that Greek was not the first Indo-European language to be spoken in Greece. This observation has important consequences for Renfrew's thesis. If Greek-speakers were not, after all, the earliest Indo-Europeans to enter Greece, it becomes very difficult to attribute the spread of Indo-European to the westward dispersion of farming folk; for there must have been not one, but at least two, distinct processes whereby Indo-European languages were introduced into Greece. Although some kind of 'cultural drift' from Anatolia to the Aegean has indeed often been postulated, this is dated to the Early Bronze Age.[13] But of course so late a 'drift' is useless to Renfrew. He would need to put back the first manifestation of Indo-European speech in Greece to a time well before the appearance of the farming folk, that is to say early in the seventh millennium. What warrant could he find for that?

A comparison of Greek with certain other Indo-European languages illustrates, even more vividly, two serious faults in Renfrew's reasoning: first in drastically over-simplifying the inter-relationships of the Indo-European languages, then in arguing for an early dispersal of Indo-European-speakers from their homeland.

---

convinced that his 'ancient European hydronymy' was of good Indo-European stock (especially in *Saeculum* 8 [1957], 1-16); but others, while accepting the correctness of Krahe's analysis in general, are sceptical of the Indo-European connexion.

13 E.g. by Schachermeyr in Die Ältesten Kulturen Griechenlands (Stuttgart 1955), 171-173, and in other publications.

Although at p. 247 of *Archaeology and Language* Renfrew alludes to 'the very early separation of the ancestors of Hittite and Greek', he shows little awareness, in general, of the complex network of resemblances which binds together the Indo-European languages in an identifiable 'family'. A closer examination of these resemblances than that conducted by Renfrew himself (see his p. 10) shows that his entire theoretical structure is unsound. The facts altogether preclude his 'vastly greater time depth, where the Indo-European antecedents of the modern European world are to be traced back six or seven thousand years, all of it on European soil' (p. 272).

That this cannot be the case is proved by well-known phenomena of Greek and Sanskrit, languages which have always formed two corner-stones of the Indo-European edifice. The pronounced similarity between Sanskrit and Greek, extending throughout much of their verbal and nominal inflexion, makes it inconceivable that the two languages developed, quite independently of each other, for thousands of years. And it is not merely a matter of conserving the same patterns of inflexion. There are some respects in which Greek and Sanskrit agree with each other against the remaining Indo-European languages. One remarkable feature of phonology is the treatment of the Indo-European syllabic nasal *$n̥$. Contrary to the development in other languages (which retain the nasal element), this sound becomes ἄ in both Greek and Sanskrit: Indo-European *$tn̥tos$, Sanskrit *tatá*, Greek τᾰτός, but Latin *tentus*, etc. In the field of morphology, Sanskrit and Greek (and only they) use an Indo-European element to form the comparative adjective (respectively -*tara*- and -τερο-). This is a significant point, relating as it does not to the common *retention* of inherited material but to the common *development* of such material, in contrast to other languages. In their vocabulary also Sanskrit and Greek sometimes show surprising correspondences. Here one may point to the parallel terms for 'word': Greek Ϝέπος beside Sanskrit *vácas*. Only Greek among the western Indo-European languages possesses such a form.

Several noun-epithet combinations were long thought to indicate that Homer and the Veda had a common ancestry in Indo-European poetry. Very few of these combinations stand uncontested to-day. Even one that used to seem unassailable, Homeric κλέος ἄφθιτον beside Vedic *ákṣitam śrávaḥ*, is unlikely to reflect directly an Indo-European antecedent.[14] In view of the uneasiness felt recently about the status of κλέος ἄφθιτον as a Homeric formula, I fear that we can hardly identify a single phrase in Homer or the Rigveda as a fragment of Indo-European poetry.[15] But

---

14 Cf. M. Finkelberg, *CQ* 36 (1986), 1-5, and E. Risch, *KZ* 100 (1987), 3-11.

15 And this despite R. Schmitt's large collection of material assembled in *Dichtung und Dichtersprache in indogermanisher Zeit* (Wiesbaden 1967).

of course the similarities between Sanskrit and Greek remain, and cannot be argued away. These similarities are, in fact, explicable only in the manner commonly proposed: the two languages, perhaps in some incipient form, remained in contact with each other for some time after the dispersal from the homeland. If we take account of the isoglosses shared by Greek with other languages (e.g. Hittite, Armenian, and Tocharian), we conclude that there must have been a highly complex series of movements.[16] To date these movements and to map them on the ground are, to my mind, impossible. But the very fact that such movements took place at all makes Renfrew's projected 'model' untenable. The sets of close resemblances between Greek and other Indo-European languages rule out the early diffusion of Indo-European speech into Greece, and so the formation of the Greek language cannot be associated with the coming of the first farmers. For reasons already given, the archaeological evidence does not suffice to date the rise of Greek more precisely; the arguments from isoglosses, however, and in particular the Greek-Sanskrit isoglosses, suggest a time between about 2500 and 1500 B.C.

---

[16] For one attempt (among many) to put these movements in chronological order, see F.R. Adrados, *Emerita* 47 (1979), 261-282.

III

THE COMING OF THE GREEKS—III

When, and in what circumstances, did the first Greek-speakers arrive in Greece? To these long-standing questions I personally believe that no final, or even provisional, answer can be given at present. But the questions themselves remain important, affecting as they do the history of the Aegean Bronze Age at a number of crucial points. From time to time a wholly or partially new proposal is made for the solution of the problem which seems to deserve special consideration—if only because it offers an alternative to the view that 'the Greeks' made their appearance at the end of the Early Bronze Age. This view has never had much to commend it positively, and within the last few decades strong reasons have emerged for rejecting it altogether.

Radically different solutions are three in number. First may be mentioned that of the late Ernst Grumach, who wished to bring in the Greeks after the Mycenaean political system had come to an end, that is to say in the twelfth century B.C. Grumach's very interesting case, which was of a linguistic or rather socio-linguistic character, I attempted to answer in

'The Coming of the Greeks', *Historia* 25, 1976, pp, 129-45. [Essay 1 in this collection.] Even if one believes, with Grumach, that the Linear B script has not yet been successfully deciphered, there remain good reasons for thinking that Greek-speakers must have been present in the Aegean region well before the end of the Bronze Age. Arguing from a diametrically opposite view-point, Colin Renfrew in *Archaeology and Language* (1987) identified the earliest Indo-European speakers in Greece with the farmers who are thought to have arrived at about 6000 B.C. On this hypothesis, Indo-European speech was introduced as part of a gradual process, not suddenly and aggressively. Although some good points are made in the course of Renfrew's discussion (chiefly on the negative side), the existence of certain linguistic facts rules out so early a date for the arrival of the Indo-Europeans. These facts I set out shortly in 'The Coming of the Greeks—II' (to appear in the forthcoming *Proceedings of the Sixth International Colloquium on Aegean Prehistory at Athens*[1]. [Essay 2 in this collection.] This third paper in the series is provoked by the publication of *The Coming of the Greeks: Indo-European Conquests in the Aegean and the Near East* by Robert Drews (1988). In his new book the distinguished author of *Basileus* advances

---

[1] In the meantime Renfrew's views have been examined in a wider context in a number of papers in *Antiquity* 62, 1988, esp. pp. 564-83, 607-9.

reasons for dating the arrival of the Greeks to about 1600. Of course this proposal is not entirely new. It was made, for instance, by W. F. Wyatt in 1970. His linguistic and archaeological conclusions are adopted by Drews and fitted into an overall historical picture.

With regard to the Indo-European homeland, which Renfrew located so confidently in eastern Anatolia, Drews is (quite rightly) cautious and undecided. He accepts the Armenian hypothesis of Gamkrelidze and Ivanov as an interesting basis for discussion, while being aware of the authors' shortcomings in several respects, especially in the interpretation (and even the understanding) of the archaeological data. But Drews' principal interest lies not in the original movements of Indo-European peoples out of their homeland. These movements, in his opinion, could not have taken the form of gradual migrations of whole peoples who in time assimilated, or were assimilated by, indigenous tribes. On the contrary, the Indo-Europeans advanced by a series of 'takeovers', whereby a comparatively small number of newcomers imposed themselves upon the native population. A new invention, the war-chariot, not only provided the Indo-Europeans with the means of establishing their superiority swiftly and effectively but also, perhaps, induced in them thoughts of conquest in the first place. In chapters 5-7 of his book, Drews traces the systematic use of horse-drawn chariots back to the seventeenth century, when the conquests of Egypt, Babylon, and Hatti were accomplished. So much, thanks to Drews' notably lucid exposition, we are entitled to regard as fact. But at this point Drews moves from fact to theory (pp. 156-7):

> I would suggest that the example of Hattusilis, and of the amurru and Hurrian princes who established their *hyksos* regimes in Egypt, may have inspired the charioteering peoples of eastern Anatolia to think new and ambitious thoughts. A community that had seen a number of its maryannu enlist to help a foreigner establish himself as lord of Hatti, or of most of Egypt, would not long have overlooked the opportunities that beckoned. It is reasonable to suggest that in the land occupied by the PIE speakers, and in neighboring lands (where, for example, Kassite and Hurrian may have been spoken), whole charioteering communities decided to wait no longer for offers of employment, but to leave home for foreign adventures and to subjugate societies more advanced but more vulnerable than their own.

What bearing have these statements of fact and opinion upon the question of the arrival of the Greeks? Simply this, that Drews regards the people buried with rich and profuse offerings in Shaft Grave Circle A at Mycenae as members of an aggressive dynasty which had established itself in Greece, so perpetrating yet another 'takeover'. That the dynasty comprised warriors who fought from horse-drawn chariots is shown by the depiction of chariots in the Shaft Graves. These observations permit Drews to propose his date of 1600 for the arrival of Greek-speakers: that is the time at which 'charioteers' were first buried in the

Shaft Graves. Such a date, reached on the witness of the monuments, is (in Drews' view) consistent with the linguistic evidence. Linguistic considerations, and also the contents of some Greek legends, lead Drews to make a further postulate, namely that the Indo-European intruders made their way first to Thessaly, and then moved southwards to subjugate other parts of Greece.

In the present short paper I shall concentrate almost exclusively upon Drews' proposals concerning the 'coming of the Greeks', since the location of the Indo-European homeland is not yet (for him or for me) beyond dispute, whereas the course of events in the Near East and Anatolia now seems fairly clear—and for the latter state of affairs we have to be grateful to Drews himself. So far as the various types of arguments concerning the 'coming of the Greeks' are concerned, I shall consider first the evidence of the Shaft Graves and the Linear B tablets, since these bulk so large in Drews' account, and then the conclusions to be drawn from the distribution of the Greek dialects.

Limiting myself to the Shaft Graves in the first instance, I notice that Drews does not deal with them in nearly so satisfactory a way as with the history of the Near East. He greatly underestimates the complexity of the problems involved in interpreting the contents of these graves, in the apparent belief that it is sufficient merely to point to one or two representations of horse-drawn chariots in order to fit the Greeks into a pattern already established for the other 'takeovers' in Egypt and the East. And those other 'takeovers' (we should be careful to note) are only associated with the use of chariots; Drews has not demonstrated, nor am I aware that any demonstration is forthcoming, that the 'takeovers' were achieved solely by the deployment of horse-drawn chariots against a native population which lacked this revolutionary means of warfare.

After these general remarks, we may turn to the graves of Circle A themselves, which are instructive for several reasons. The objects discovered in the six graves are, naturally, of the greatest importance; but the stelae and fragments of stelae are significant as well; and the very arrangements of the graves may be suggestive.

To start with the first-mentioned point. The use of a small number of neighbouring graves, of a similar type and having a similar orientation, over a short period (perhaps three generations or so) means, in all likelihood, that they form the cemetery of a single dynasty—however widely we may choose to interpret this term. That it was a 'royal' dynasty we cannot doubt, in view of the richness of the deposits in some graves; and the later inhabitants of Mycenae seem to have considered the dynasty more than royal, to judge from their reverence for, and reconstruction of, the whole Circle.

When Kato compiled his great catalogue of, and commentary on, the Shaft Graves and their contents in *Die Schachtgräber von Mykenai* (1930-3), he could point to little by way of parallels or antecedents. For him, as previously for Schliemann, the gravegoods (especially those of the richest tombs, IV and V) were an astounding phenomenon, attesting the sudden acquisition of vast wealth and the equally sudden discovery of far wider horizons than had been known to previous inhabitants of Greece. The world of the 'Shaft Grave kings', as we have to call them, embraced (at the very least) Crete, the Cyclades, the Near East, Anatolia, and northern Europe. It has to be admitted that the source of wealth in the Shaft Graves and the reasons for such extensive foreign involvement are still completely obscure. Nevertheless post-war discoveries, both at Mycenae and in Messenia, have made the Shaft Graves and their contents less isolated in the history of Greece than was the case in the time of Karo.

In Messenia the relevant sites are Peristeria and Pylos. A small grave circle, lying south-east of the area of the later palace of Pylos, contained at least four burial-pits. The pits and their environs yielded a variety of objects resembling, more or less closely, their counterparts in the Shaft Graves. These resemblances, which apply particularly to gold and silver ornaments, cauldrons, rapiers of Karo's Type A, and a knife (all in bronze), a whetstone, an ivory pommel, amber beads, and boar's tusks, are pointed out by the excavator[2]. The gold diadem in Pit 4,

---

2 W. D. Taylour in *The Palace of Nestor* III, 1973, pp. 134-76.

though recalling the decoration on the much larger diadems in the Shaft Graves, finds its closest parallel at Peristeria.

The Peristeria cemetery contained tholoi, which are important from an architectural point of view, and a shaft of irregular shape, the significance of which lies in the burial-offerings[3]. The offerings, many of them of gold or gold leaf, have been described by Korres and compared by him with Shaft Grave types, which they closely resemble[4]. The objects with the most striking parallels in the Shaft Graves are a diadem, a cup decorated with spirals and circles, pieces of foil cut out in the shape of flowers and birds: all in gold[5]. The contents of the Peristeria tomb are the richest yet known from this period outside Mycenae. Not only Argolis, therefore, but Messenia also began to have access to sources of wealth previously unexploited. Wherever the people of Mycenae and Peristeria got their gold, they made it into ornaments and utensils; many of these are purely native work, owing neither their decoration nor manner of construction to any external region[6]. Now Drews takes note of the Peristeria material, and appreciates how closely some

---

[3] The cemetery was excavated by S. Marinatos and re-excavated by G. S. Korres: respectively *Praktika*, 1965, pp. 102-20 and *Praktika*, 1976, pp. 469-550.

[4] *Praktika*, 1976, pp. 486-501.

[5] S. Iakovidis, *TUAS* 6, 1981, pp. 17-28.

[6] B. Kling, *TUAS* 6, 1981, pp. 29-38.

of it resembles objects in the Mycenae Shaft Graves (p. 186). He does not, however, explain how the native workmanship evident at Peristeria can be reconciled with the 'sixteenth century takeover' of the Messenian coast.

Turning back to Mycenae itself, we have to bring into the discussion Grave Circle B, which occupies a burial-area outside the citadel. Prolonged study of the tombs of Circle B, and especially of their contents, has established a number of points. First a matter of chronology[7]. Circle B came into use earlier than Schliemann's Circle A but overlapped it in time, with the latest interments being made in B while the earliest depositions were taking place in A[8]. It would be interesting, but not very rewarding, to speculate on the reasons which led to the construction of a new grave circle and the abandonment of the old. Of greater importance is the recognition that both circles participate in the same material culture and that this culture has its roots in the Greek mainland. The pottery, as usual, provides the most persuasive index of cultural continuity. Middle Helladic ware is found

---

[7] The excavator, I. Papadimitriou, regarded it as possible, but not certain, that B incorporates elements of a still earlier circle: *Praktika*, 1954, p. 263.

[8] G. E. Mylonas, Ὁ Ταφικὸς Κύκλος Β τῶν Μυκηνῶν 1973, p. 355; F. Schachermeyr, *Die mykenische Zeit und die Gesittung von Thera*, 1976, pp. 228-32; O. T. P. K. Dickinson, *The Origins of Mycenaean Civilisation*, 1977, pp. 50-51; G. Graziado, *AJA* 92, 1988, pp. 343-72.

in the earliest graves of Circle B as well as in the latest of Circle A. The Minoanizing pottery known as Late Helladic I sometimes accompanies the Middle Helladic ware in Circle A but does not supplant it. A close affinity is found in other types of objects, such as the death-masks, engraved gems, and gold cups; also the ornaments of various shapes in gold leaf, which (as already stated) have no good parallels outside Greece. A final link between the two circles is provided by the practice of erecting stelae over the graves; and the manner of decorating the stelae is in some cases very similar, as one may see by comparing Mylonas' Γ 491 (Circle B) with Karo's nos. 1428 and 1429 (Circle A).

It is therefore now possible to accept without reserve Karo's identification of a continuing Helladic strand in Circle A[9] but also to acknowledge that this strand can be traced back to the earlier circle[10]. We must not allow this fact to be obscured by the intensification of Minoan influence, the growing emphasis on weaponry (not, of course, that weapons are absent from Circle B), and the barbaric splendour and opulence displayed by some graves, especially III, IV, and V in Circle A.

The persistence of the Helladic element throughout both grave circles is not fully appreciated by Drews. In one place he speaks almost as if the discoveries in

---

9 *Schachtgräber*, p. 342.

10 Mylonas, *op. cit.*, pp. 358-62.

Circle B and at Peristeria had never been made or, if made, had not been understood (p. 23):

> What suggests that they [the people buried in Circle A] might have been newcomers to Greece, freshly arrived from the land of the PIE speakers, is the fact that the deposits found in the shaft graves seem to be without precedent at Mycenae or anywhere else in Greece. The more archaeologists have learned about the Middle Helladic period, the more convinced some observers have become that no evolution or gradual progress led up to the bellicose opulence of the Shaft Grave Dynasty.[11]

It is true that, if one had only the evidence of Circle B, the range and richness of offerings in Circle A would have been impossible to predict; but, with our knowledge of both circles we can follow certain basic trends, without ever (I hope) losing our sense of wonder at the array of treasures brought to light by Schliemann in Circle A. Later in his book Drews takes the question of pottery into special consideration (p. 178):

> The argument that the Shaft grave Dynasty was indigenous to the Argolid, and that Middle Helladic Greece evolved into late Helladic Greece without interruption or invasion, depends entirely on pottery: the absence of an intruder's ware and the persistence of local wares. Much is made of the fact that from the clay pots

---

[11] Who these observers are, is not stated. Only one is named.

found in the two grave circles a continuum can be traced from Middle to Late Helladic shapes and motifs. This is, of course, true (although the progress from the drab Middle Helladic wares to the striking, Minoanized pottery of the Late Helladic period is more revolutionary than evolutionary), but ceramic continuity says nothing about the provenance of the shaft-grave dynasts. Pottery was one of the least significant artifacts in the shaft-grave corredo...The dynasts were charioteers and not potters, and it is hardly surprising that their pottery, like other humble necessities of daily life, should have been supplied to them by the subject population.

Of course the natives could have gone on making their traditional types of pottery even after the arrival of the postulated dynasty of charioteers who, in their lordly way, had other things to occupy their attention than the fabrication of pots. But what is hardly conceivable is that when the 'charioteers' took possession of the place they introduced nothing new (except, of course, the chariot) but simply adopted the modes of working which were, and had long been, in use among the indigenous population. When did conquerors ever behave like this? Only if they had no culture of their own, or none worth preserving, and were content to embrace the higher civilization. But that is not the course of events imagined by Drews. He thinks of a new aristocracy, forcing their way into Greece because of their mastery of a new instrument of war. He goes so far as to call the occupants of Circle A 'charioteers' (p. 178 and elsewhere). But on what evidence?

In Grave Circle A the depictions of chariots number only four: the stelae 1428 and 1429 in Karo's numeration (what the scenes exactly represent is a matter of dispute, but there can be no doubt that a light, horse-drawn chariot is shown), the fragment of a stele illustrated in Karo's pl. X (bottom left-hand corner), and the gold ring from Grave IV (Karo's no. 240), a drawing of which is found on the jacket of *The Coming of the Greeks*. These representations, few as they are and (with the exception of the gold ring) difficult to interpret, undoubtedly point to some knowledge of the chariot on the artists' part: they hardly justify Drews in constantly referring to the people buried in Circle A as 'charioteers'. That is to place altogether undue weight upon evidence of one type at the expense of the rest. Among the objects buried with the dead in Circle A the swords, rapiers, and daggers stand out in quality and quantity. And when we observe that the two principal types of the forty swords in this circle continue the types already represented (by sixteen examples) in Circle B, we may infer that the warriors preferred close combat to chariot-fighting—furthermore that this predilection is typical of Circle A no less than of Circle B.

For such reasons I believe that the depictions of chariots in Circle A have been invested with a significance they do not really possess. The people buried in the Shaft Graves should not be called 'charioteers'; nor do they represent an entirely new and revolutionary element in the population of Greece.

How the Shaft Grave people came by their knowledge of the chariot we cannot tell. Karo, who seems to have been no less aware than Drews of the decisive part played by chariots in the conquest of Babylon and Egypt, declined to assign them so important a role in Greece and suggested that the Mycenaeans learnt about them from the Hittites[12]. In other words, it was only after the Shaft Grave dynasty had acquired their wealth (however they did acquire it) and had engaged in their vastly increased intercourse with other regions that they came by knowledge of the chariot. It is in any case most unlikely that, in the seventeenth century or subsequently, chariots could have been so effectively deployed in the Argolid as upon the plains of Egypt and the Middle East. But Drews believes that the occupants of the Shaft Graves not merely comprised a new and aggressive dynasty who had seized Mycenae by force but were also the first speakers of Indo-European to enter Greece. In support of this view, he adduces two linguistic arguments, which may now be considered.

Drews' first argument (p 117):

indicates that the Greek language and the chariot arrived in Greece at the same time, which is to say that the chariot was brought to Greece by Indo-European invaders. More conservatively stated, as Wyatt does in his meticulous and concise article, the argument holds

---

[12] *Schachtgräber*, p. 338.

that 'the Greeks' could not have come to Greece before they made an acquaintance with the chariot. The argument is based on a linguistic generalization: if a language includes an inherited word with its original meaning, then the object denoted by the word must have been 'constantly and continuously known' to the speakers of that language. If, then, we find the early Greeks citing Indo-European (or 'Greek') terms for a new contraption that arrived in Greece ca. 1600 B.C., we may conclude either that the Indo-Europeans (or 'Greeks') arrived at the same time as the contraption, or that they arrived at a later date (having in the meantime become acquainted elsewhere with the chariot). At any rate 'the Greeks' cannot have been living in Greece before the innovation occurred.

Since the stages of this argument are not set out by Drews himself, it is necessary to refer back to Wyatt's paper[13]. That this is a 'meticulous and concise article' I have no wish to deny; but, unlike Drews, I am not convinced by the author's thesis. The reasons follow.

Wyatt states (and I agree with him) that 'the best place to begin our search for areas of meaning containing Indo-European elements is clearly the earliest source of information concerning Greek, namely the Linear B tablets'[14]. The first piece of

---

13 "The Indo-Europeanization of Greece" *in Indo-European and Indo-Europeans,* ed. G. Cardona, H. M. Hoenigswalk, A. Senn, 1970, pp. 89-111.

14 *Op. cit.,* p.100.

evidence adduced is the Knossos tablet now numbered
Sd 4403:

.b [i-]qi-ja a-ja-me-na e-re-pa-te a-ra-ro-mo-te-me-na
a-ra-ru-ja [a-ni-ja-pi]

.a e-re-pa-te-jo o-po-qo ke-ra-ja-pi o-pi-i-ja-pi 'ko-ki-
da o-pa'

Wheel-Less Chariots 3

The relevant items of vocabulary are discussed by
Wyatt as follows. *i-qi-ja* is clearly a derivative of *i-qo*
(ἵππος 'horse'), and doubtless here means 'horse-
chariot'. It is to be taken as an adjectival form,
probably modifying a *wo-ka* which has to be
understood; this word is actually found on the Pylos
wheel-tablets (to which we shall return later). 'The fact
that *i-qi-ja*, an adjective, is used indicates that there
was some other type of *wo-ka* available in Mycenaean
times, and that *wo-ka* would almost certainly have
been one drawn by mules'[15]. Postponing for a moment
discussion of *i-qi-ja*, we notice that *a-ni-ja-pi*, restored
on this tablet by the editors, is found after *a-ra-ru-ja* in
other texts of the set. It is the instrumental of a word
meaning 'reins' or 'bridle' (i.e. ἄνιᾱφι: 'Indo-European
connections for this word are not altogether certain,
but are probable'[16]. Two cognates are suggested,
Sanskrit *nāsyam* and Irish *e(i)si* (< *ansio-*); it is
hardly possible for *both* to be right, and the connexion

---

[15] *Op. cit.*, p.100.

[16] *Op. cit.*, pp. 100-1.

of either with Greek ἀνίαι has never been demonstrated in a cogent manner. 'o-po-qo is not certainly interpreted... o-pi-i-ja-pi is even less securely identified than the other words'[17]. Where the author himself has so little confidence in the Indo-European relationship, we shall not feel more secure. It turns out, on Wyatt's own showing, that the only term in the Sd tablets which is indubitably of Indo-European origin is the word for 'chariot' itself, i-qi-ja.

A number of tablets from Pylos, mentioned by Wyatt, scarcely help his case. Ub 1315, for example, speaks of a-pu-ke in the same context as a-ni-ja; this a-pu-ke no doubt represents a form of ἄμπυξ, in which an Indo-European stem has been discerned, 'but this connection is not sufficiently specific to chariots to prove an Indo-European origin of this part of the harness arrangements'[18]. Wyatt says that the leather object destined for ti-ri-si ze-u-ke-si (Ub 1318.4) refers to a two-horse chariot[19] but, while the element is unquestionably of Indo-European origin, the 'yoke' of animals need not refer to a two-horse chariot, or even (without further specification) to horses at all. The Mycenaean words for 'wheel' (a-mo) and 'axles' (a-ko-so-ne) are rightly seen as Indo-European derivatives; on the other band, there is nothing to show that they are the wheels and axles of chariots.

---

[17] Op. cit., p.101.

[18] Op. cit., p.102.

[19] Op. cit., p.102.

The last of the Linear B items in Wyatt's list is *wo-ka*. He (like many others) interprets PY Sa 834 as a record of wheels for a chariot, the word for a chariot here being *wo-ka*:

a-me-ja-to wo-ka we-je-ke-e WHEEL + TE ZE 1

If *wo-ka* represents Ϝοχά and is (as Wyatt maintains) continued by Homeric ὄχος, a link with Indo-European **wegh-* seems inescapable. Even so, *wo-ka* need denote only a 'conveyance'; there is nothing in the Sa set which indicates it is a 'war-chariot'. In fact, however, a completely different approach to the interpretation of this set should be envisaged.[20]

The word *i-qi-ja* remains. Its Indo-European credentials are undeniable. But by what means does this particular form convey the meaning 'horse-drawn chariot'? In a commentary on the chariot-tablets written not long after Ventris' decipherment, Chantraine suggested that *i-qi-ja* represents a feminine noun, perhaps collective in origin, of the same type as οἰκίᾱ, ἡνίᾱ, etc.[21] This explanation, in my own belief, offers the best hope of understanding the formation of *i-qi-ja*. A 'collection' of horses and equipment is thereby expressed by means of a feminine well attested in Greek: thus ἱππία would be

----

20   This is also the belief of Y. Duhoux, *Aspects du vocabulaire économique mycénien*, 1976, pp. 126-8.

21   P. Chantraine, *Minos* 4, 1956, p.63.

based on ἵππος, as οἰκία is based on οἶκος, ἡνία on ἤνια, κλισία on κλισίον, ἑστία on a ἑστο-, κοπρία on κόπρος, and so on. Furthermore, if ἱππία is interpreted in this 'collective' sense, it finds a close parallel in the Homeric use of ἵπποι(or dual ἵππω) to designate not just a team of horses but the whole assemblage: horses plus chariot. It is thus disappointing to find that in a later paper Chantraine preferred to regard *i-qi-ja* as an adjectival form, with a *wo-ka* understood[22]. This is the interpretation favoured by other writers on the subject, e.g. Chadwick, Lejeune, Ruijgh (but not Palmer). But, as we have seen, the interpretation is open to question, partly because *wo-ka* cannot be shown positively to mean 'chariot' (or even, if Duhoux is right, to have any connexion with **wegh-*), partly because it is after all mere surmise that *wo-ka* and not some other word has to be understood, finally because Greek usage points to a collective, substantival meaning of *i-qi-ja*.

But, however the formation of *i-qi-ja* is to be explained, no one disputes the association with *i-qo*, 'horse'. This very association makes for a serious, though unacknowledged difficulty in the theory propounded by Wyatt and, after him, by Drews. For whether ἱππία is a collective noun based upon ἵππος or an adjective qualifying some feminine noun which has to be understood, it is a secondary formation, not a word brought to Greece by the first Indo-European-

---

[22] *RPh* 38, 1964, p. 262.

speakers. What *they* brought was ἵππος. The use of ἱππίᾱ in the sense of 'chariot' came later; how much later, we do not know. It is only if horse *and* chariot arrived together that Wyatt's argument would carry much weight; far from marking the horse-drawn chariot as an invention introduced into Greece at the same time as its name, the word ἱππίᾱ suggests (it does not prove) that the chariot was discovered only after ἵππος had become established as a Greek word.

Drews' other argument from language can, perhaps, be discussed more briefly. He accepts (as I think we all must) the proposition that the historical Greek dialects were created within Greece and that the process of creation owed nothing to further incursions of Indo-European-speakers. And when Drews follows Risch in postulating a more conservative ('South Greek') dialect during the Bronze Age (p. 39), that also is a reasonable assumption on the facts. But further conclusions drawn by Drews are, in my mind, unwarranted. He seems to envisage a situation in late Mycenaean times in which there was, practically speaking, only one dialect in northern Greece and only one in southern Greece; moreover, 'speakers of North and South Greek were more readily intelligible to each other in the twelfth century B.C. than were Dorians and Ionians in the seventh century B.C.' (pp. 40-1). Such large claims are without foundation. Of North Greek we know nothing, except that it had not changed *ti* to *si*. All we know of South Greek is what we read in the Linear B tablets; and even the highly standardized official language written there reveals some dialectal differences, as Risch himself has shown[23]. Risch was, in any case, careful to speak of a South Greek 'dialect area' (Dialekt-raum)[24]; and analogy would suggest that the 'dialect-areas' of Mycenaean Greece were not sharply demarcated from each other but that, for instance, some 'northern' features were found in some 'South Greek' dialects, and *vice versa*. When we observe the high degree of cultural homogeneity achieved by the late Mycenaean period, we may assume that there must have been frequent and close contact between the major centres and this intercourse led to a blurring of linguistic boundaries. In this situation, I see little sense in speculating to what extent the two groups were mutually intelligible, none in asserting that they were more intelligible than other groups centuries later. These speculations reveal nothing about the date of the Indo-European arrival in Greece.

The two foundations upon which Drews built his case for an incursion of Indo-European chariot-drivers into Greece at the beginning of the seventeenth century have now been examined: these are, respectively, archaeological and linguistic. For the reasons given, they do not seem, even in combination, sufficient to bear the burden of proof. On the other hand, despite the lack of positive support for the arrival of Indo-

---

[23] E. Risch in *The Cambridge Colloquium on Mycenaean Studies*, 1966, pp. 150-7 = *Kleine Schriften*, 1981, pp. 451-8.

[24] *MH* 12, 1955, p. 70 = *Kleine Schriften*, p. 215.

European-speakers early in the Mycenaean age, it remains possible that they did enter Greece at that time; although in circumstances other than those suggested by Drews. His further arguments (partly from archaeology, partly from language, partly from legend) involve Thessaly and tend to show that this region formed a stage on the journey of the first Indo-European-speakers into southern Greece (pp. 191-4). The argument from legend is certainly quite strong, but only to the extent that it emphasizes the Thessalian contribution to the earliest cycles; although this contribution may indeed suggest a *route* possibly followed by the earliest Greek-speakers, it conveys nothing about the date or manner of their arrival. The same is true of the archaeological and linguistic arguments which are, however, considerably weaker than the deductions from legend.